Amy Lippman

D1545661

Challenge to Confirmands

Challenge

SCRIBE PUBLICATIONS, Inc., New York

TO CONFIRMANDS

An Introduction to Jewish Thinking

ARNOLD JACOB WOLF

Copyright © 1963 by Arnold Jacob Wolf

All rights reserved, including those of translation and reproduction of this book or portions thereof in any form.

Second Edition

Library of Congress Catalog Card Number 63-20184

Published by Scribe Publications, Inc., New York
Manufactured in the United States of America

Acknowledgments

The author wishes to thank the following authors and publishers for graciously permitting him to quote from works published by them.

Reprinted by permission of:

Abelard-Schuman Ltd.
 The Earth is the Lord's by Abraham J. Heschel, copyright 1950
Bloch Publishing Co.
 The Hertz Daily Siddur
 A Guide for Reform Jews, copyright by Frederic Doppelt and David
  Polish
 The Place of Understanding, copyright by Jacob Weinstein
Duell, Sloan & Pearce, an affiliate of Meredith Press
 The Jew in Our Day, copyright, 1944, by Waldo Frank
E. P. Dutton & Co., Inc.
 Everyman's Talmud by The Rev. Dr. A. Cohen
Europäische Verlagsanstalt GmbH.
 Dieses Volk by Leo Baeck
Farrar, Strauss & Cudahy, Inc.
 At the Turning Point, copyright, 1952, by Martin Buber
 Judaism and Modern Man, copyright, 1951, by Will Herberg
 God in Search of Man, copyright, 1955, by Abraham J. Heschel
 Man is not Alone, copyright, 1951, by Abraham J. Heschel
Harper & Row, Publishers, Inc.
 To Hallow this Life by Martin Buber, Editor Jacob Trapp
 Eclipse of God by Martin Buber
Harcourt, Brace & World, Inc.
 Basic Judaism, copyright, 1947, by Milton Steinberg
Hebrew Publishing Co.
 Maimonides, "Guide for the Perplexed"
Jewish Frontier
 The Inner Eye by Hayim Greenberg
Jewish Publication Society
 Judaism and Christianity by Leo Baeck
 Judaism and Modern Man, copyright, 1951, by Will Herberg
 Man is not Alone, copyright, 1951, by Abraham J. Heschel
 God in Search of Man, copyright, 1955, by Abraham J. Heschel

Mekilta, Vol. II, by M. Lauterbach
A Rabbinic Anthology by Claude G. Montefiore and H. Loewe
Jewish Reconstructionist Foundation, Inc.
  Toward a Guide for Jewish Ritual Usage
The Macmillan Company
  Jewish Theology by Kaufmann Kohler, copyright, 1946, by Lili Kohler
  Where Judaism Differed by Abba Hillel Silver
Macmillan & Co. Ltd.
  Outlines of Liberal Judaism by Claude G. Montefiore
Mentor Books, New American Library
  The Living Talmud by Judah Goldin
Philosophical Library, Publishers
  Legacy of Maimonides by Ben Zion Bokser
Schocken Books, Inc.
  Tales of the Hasidim, The Early Masters by Martin Buber, copyright,
    1947, by Schocken Books, Inc.
  Tales of the Hasidim, The Later Masters by Martin Buber, copyright,
    1948, by Schocken Books, Inc.
  Franz Rosenzweig by Nahum N. Glatzer, copyright, 1953, 1961, by
    Schocken Books, Inc.
  Franz Rosenzweig-Briefe, copyright, 1935, by Schocken Verlag, Berlin
  In Time and Eternity by Nahum N. Glatzer, copyright, 1946, by Schocken
    Books, Inc.
Scribner's
  Man's Quest for God, copyright by Abraham J. Heschel
U.A.H.C.
  God and Man in Judaism by Leo Baeck
  What We Jews Believe by Samuel S. Cohon
    copyright by The Union of American Hebrew Congregations
The United Synagogue of America
  From David Aronson's *The Jewish Way of Life* (New York, 1957), a
    publication of the National Academy for Adult Jewish Studies of the
    United Synagogue of America
Yale University Press
  The Midrash on Psalms by William Braude

Contents

A Dedication

Once, at parting, the Baal Shem blessed his student.
Then he bowed his own head to receive the blessing
from him. Rabbi Baer drew back, but the Baal Shem
took his hand and laid it on his head.

CHAPTER ONE

What Must a Jew Believe?

To be a Jew is to be free. One of Judaism's best advertised advantages is freedom, the right to think things out in our own way for ourselves. We Jews do not feel bound to accept or believe anything very specific. Our consciences are absolutely our own. Jews are divided into many schools of thought, nearly all of which concede that the others are really Jews though they may be mistaken Jews. Even within liberal Judaism itself there are many different beliefs, some directly contradicting others. Yet people who disagree belong to the same congregation, pray from the same prayer book, learn from the same rabbi. Though we differ, we can be very important to each other. And this, too, is a mark of our freedom.

Milton Steinberg, a great American rabbi who died in 1950, summarized the reasons for asserting the freedom of Jews to believe as they wish. There are three reasons at least, he said, why Judaism cannot be said to have a creed, a fixed statement of belief to which every true Jew must give assent:

> We hold that Judaism cannot be a creedal religion, and that for three reasons:
>
> First, if Judaism has dogmas, where are they? Why were they never formulated officially, not even in the days when authoritative bodies existed capable of formulating and imposing them? Why, for example, did the Sanhedrin during seven hundred years of spiritual predominance never publish a set of articles of Jewish faith?
>
> Second, no draft of the Jewish creed attempted by any individual has ever won universal acceptance, not even the Thirteen Principles of Faith drawn up by Moses Maimonides, the undisputed master of all medieval Jewish theologians. For though at the present time most Orthodox Jews view the Maimonidean creed with great reverence, every article in it has been challenged by someone or another, and more than an occasional Jew is a critic of it to this day.
>
> Third, Jews cannot share a set of dogmas for the very simple but compelling reason that they have never been of one mind on theological matters. The Bible itself discloses diversities in religious outlook. The sages of the Talmud are surprisingly variegated in their convictions. Doctrinal difference has always been the rule among professing Jews; it is the rule more sweepingly in modern times.

But, we must ask, is our freedom to agree or dissent an absolute freedom? Is there nothing at all that Jews must believe? If there is really nothing, then Judaism becomes vague, so personal that it would be invented all over again by each Jew. If there is nothing we must believe, then is Judaism only whatever we want it to be? Rabbi Steinberg gives three countervailing reasons

for thinking that Judaism must have dogmas, beliefs
that are required of every Jew:

> To say that Judaism has no dogmas is absurd.
> First, it is to assert of the Jewish religion that it stands
> for nothing in particular, that it is a jellyfish of a faith.
> Second, if Judaism has no distinctive convictions, what
> kept the Jews together through their long and stormy
> history? What was it for which Jewish martyrs died?
> Third, Judaism has from time to time taken firm
> stands against ideas current in the world about itself.

The question of requirements is a difficult one indeed. As you will see throughout this book, most important questions are complicated and controversial.
In some churches, dogmas are exact and obligatory.
Beliefs have the power to open heaven to the believer.
One who denies the dogmas of the Catholic catechism
is in danger of losing eternal life, according to that very
catechism. Judaism does not seem to have any dogmas
in that sense of the word. Jews have disagreed among
themselves too long and too vigorously to presume to
keep other Jews out of heaven, at least with any real
hope of success.

And yet, throughout the history of Judaism, some
authorities have tried to set forth beliefs required of
every Jew, in addition to the 613 commandments
which every Jew was expected to obey. One of the
oldest of these "creeds" is found in the Mishnah, the
earliest part of the Talmud written shortly after the
time of Jesus. The rabbis of the Mishnah believed that
all Jews and all righteous people everywhere would
have a share in the "coming world," a heavenly future

for mankind both on this earth and in the other world. Everyone would inherit this future joy, they insisted, except a few heretical Jews who denied the basic principles of Judaism as the Mishnah thought of them. Here is what the Mishnah says:

> All Israelites have a share in the coming world except these who do not:
>
> 1. The person who denies that the Torah teaches the revival of the dead.
> 2. The person who denies that the Torah came from Heaven.
> 3. The unbeliever.
> 4. According to Rabbi Akiba, also the person who reads secular books.
> 5. The person who tries to cure disease with magic.
> 6. Abba Saul adds: the person who pronounces God's name irreverently.

The most difficult term to understand in this Mishnah is the word "unbeliever" which probably means something like "atheist" or "cynic." He is the man who is suspicious about whether Judaism is basically right at all. The "unbeliever" seems to have thought himself out of the Jewish religion, and cannot therefore participate in its eternal future. In any case, the Talmudic rabbis believed that there was something, at least, which Jews had to believe or pay for rejecting it.

Philo, a Jewish philosopher of about the same time who lived in Alexandria, listed five dogmas that he thought a Jew must believe:

1. There is a God who rules the world.
2. God is one.
3. God created the world.

6

4. The world is orderly and harmonious.
5. God rules all and cares for all.

Maimonides, the greatest Jewish philosopher who lived in the twelfth century, summarized in thirteen famous principles what he thought a Jew should accept. His creed is often printed in traditional Jewish prayer books and, though it raised a tremendous controversy during the Middle Ages, it is now generally accepted by Orthodox Jews.

1. I believe with perfect faith that the Creator, blessed be His Name, is the Author and Guide of everything that has been created, and that He alone has made, does make, and will make all things.
2. I believe with perfect faith that the Creator, blessed be His Name, is a Unity, and that there is no unity in any manner like His, and that He alone is our God, who was, is, and will be.
3. I believe with perfect faith that the Creator, blessed be His Name, is not a body, and that He is free from all the properties of matter, and that He has not any form whatsoever.
4. I believe with perfect faith that the Creator, blessed be His Name, is the first and the last.
5. I believe with perfect faith that to the Creator, blessed be His Name, and to Him alone, it is right to pray, and that it is not right to pray to any being besides Him.
6. I believe with perfect faith that all the words of the prophets are true.
7. I believe with perfect faith that the prophecy of Moses, our teacher, peace be unto him, was true, and that he was the chief of the prophets, both of those that preceded and of those that followed.
8. I believe with perfect faith that the whole Torah, now in our possession, is the same that was given to Moses, our teacher, peace be unto him.

9. I believe with perfect faith that this Torah will not be changed, and that there will never be any other Law from the Creator, blessed be His Name.

10. I believe with perfect faith that the Creator, blessed be His Name, knows every deed of the children of men, and all their thoughts.

11. I believe with perfect faith that the Creator, blessed be His Name, rewards those that keep His Commandments, and punishes those that transgress them.

12. I believe with perfect faith in the coming of the Messiah; and, though he delay, I will wait daily for his coming.

13. I believe with perfect faith that there will be a revival of the dead at the time when it shall please the Creator, blessed be His Name, and exalted be His fame for ever and ever.

The first five articles of Maimonides' Creed are about God: they assert that He is the only Creator, one, immaterial, primary and the only true object of our prayer. The next four articles are about the Torah: it is true, lasting and unchangeable—especially the five books of Moses. The last four articles deal with the Providence and Retribution of God who will bring the Messiah to redeem the world, and call the dead back to life, rewarding the good and punishing the evil. It might be well for you to look carefully at each of these beliefs to see how they square with your own convictions. Clearly some of them, like the unity of God, are much more congenial to most of us than others, like the doctrine of the unchanging Torah.

But even in the time of Maimonides there were other opinions. Joseph Albo, a Jewish philosopher who lived a little later, thought about the kind of dogmas that all religions have. Every religion has "root" beliefs, according to Albo, and these "roots" are the same for all religions. From the "roots" spring "stems" which are different in the several religions, but which are required of the man who accepts any particular faith. In addition to the "stems" there are "branches" which are unique to each religion and do not have the importance of the "roots" and "stems." How is it with the Jewish tree?

> The "roots" of Judaism, as of every revealed religion, are three: The *Existence of God, Revelation,* and *Retribution.* The special character of each religion shows itself in the "stems" and "branches" that grow out of the "roots." In the case of Judaism, the first root of God's Existence produces four stems: *God's unity, incorporeality, timelessness,* and *perfection.* The root of Retribution has two stems: *divine omniscience* and *providence.* In addition to the three roots and eight stems, Judaism has six branches, or beliefs, which, while not fundamental to Judaism, every Jew is expected to believe. They are: *creation,* the superiority of *Moses* over all prophets, eternity of the *Torah* of Moses, possibility of attaining to human *perfection* through the proper observance of even one commandment, *resurrection,* and the *Messiah.*

Kaufmann Kohler, the greatest theologian of Reform Judaism in America, summarized five similar beliefs which he considered absolutely necessary to Judaism this way:

1. There is a God.
2. God has revealed His will to man.
3. This is a moral world in which good is rewarded and evil punished in the end.
4. There is a life after death.
5. There will be a Messianic time on earth.

In Columbus, Ohio, in 1937, the entire Conference of Reform Rabbis adopted a set of "Guiding Principles of Reform Judaism." The purpose of these principles was not to require any belief, but rather to "guide" liberal Jews toward a fuller understanding and a clearer appreciation of what Reform Judaism stands for. Even this goal was opposed by many rabbis. They feared that the guide might become a catechism. Others, however, insisted that a changing Judaism needs re-statement of conviction over and over again; even if Judaism is constantly changing, there must be something significant which does the changing. When the rabbis voted on the Columbus Platform, the vote was an exact tie. The President of the Conference, Felix A. Levy, broke the tie in favor of the setting-forth of these principles which, since that time, have had considerable impact on American Judaism.

I. JUDAISM AND ITS FOUNDATIONS

1. *Nature of Judaism.* Judaism is the historical religious experience of the Jewish people. Though growing out of Jewish life, its message is universal, aiming at the union and perfection of mankind under the sovereignty of God. Reform Judaism recognizes the principle of progressive development in religion and consciously applies this principle to spiritual as well as to cultural and social life.

Judaism welcomes all truth, whether written in the pages of scripture or deciphered from the records of nature. The new discoveries of science, while replacing the older scientific views underlying our sacred literature, do not conflict with the essential spirit of religion as manifested in the consecration of man's will, heart and mind to the service of God and of humanity.

2. *God.* The heart of Judaism and its chief contribution to religion is the doctrine of the One, living God, who rules the world through law and love. In Him all existence has its creative source and mankind its ideal of conduct. Though transcending time and space, He is the indwelling Presence of the world. We worship Him as the Lord of the Universe and as our merciful Father.

3. *Man.* Judaism affirms that man is created in the Divine image. His spirit is immortal. He is an active co-worker with God. As a child of God, he is endowed with moral freedom and is charged with the responsibility of overcoming evil and striving after ideal ends.

4. *Torah.* God reveals Himself not only in the majesty, beauty and orderliness of nature, but also in the vision and moral striving of the human spirit. Revelation is a continuous process, confined to no one group and to no one age. Yet the people of Israel, through its prophets and sages, achieved unique insight in the realm of religious truth. The Torah, both written and oral, enshrines Israel's ever-growing consciousness of God and of the moral law. It preserves the historical precedents, sanctions and norms of Jewish life, and seeks to mould it in the patterns of goodness and of holiness. Being products of historical processes, certain of its laws have lost their binding force with the passing of the conditions that called them forth. But as a depository of permanent spiritual ideals, the Torah remains the dynamic source of the life of Israel. Each age has the obligation to adapt the teachings of the Torah to its basic needs in consonance with the genius of Judaism.

5. *Israel.* Judaism is the soul of which Israel is the body. Living in all parts of the world, Israel has been held together by the ties of a common history, and above all, by the heritage of faith. Though we recognize in the group-loyalty of Jews who have become estranged from our religious tradition, a bond which still unites them with us, we maintain that it is by its religion and for its religion that the Jewish people has lived. The non-Jew who accepts our faith is welcomed as a full member of the Jewish community.

In all lands where our people live, they assume and seek to share loyally the full duties and responsibilities of citizenship and to create seats of Jewish knowledge and religion. In the rehabilitation of Palestine, the land hallowed by memories and hopes, we behold the promise of renewed life for many of our brethren. We affirm the obligation of all Jewry to aid in its upbuilding as a Jewish homeland by endeavoring to make it not only a haven of refuge for the oppressed but also a center of Jewish culture and spiritual life.

Throughout the ages it has been Israel's mission to witness to the Divine in the face of every form of paganism and materialism. We regard it as our historic task to cooperate with all men in the establishment of the kingdom of God, of universal brotherhood, justice, truth and peace on earth. This is our Messianic goal.

II. ETHICS

6. *Ethics and Religion.* In Judaism religion and morality blend into an indissoluble unity. Seeking God means to strive after holiness, righteousness and goodness. The love of God is incomplete without the love of one's fellowmen. Judaism emphasizes the kinship of the human race, the sanctity and worth of human life and personality and the right of the individual to freedom and to the pursuit of his chosen vocation. Justice to all, irrespective of race, sect or class is the inalienable right and the inescapable obligation of all. The state and organized government exist in order to further these ends.

7. *Social Justice.* Judaism seeks the attainment of a just society by the application of its teachings to the economic order, to industry and commerce, and to national and international affairs. It aims at the elimination of man-made misery and suffering, of poverty and degradation, of tyranny and slavery, of social inequality and prejudice, of ill-will and strife. It advocates the promotion of harmonious relations between warring classes on the basis of equity and justice, and the creation of conditions under which human personality may flourish. It pleads for the safeguarding of childhood against exploitation. It champions the cause of all who work and of their right to an adequate standard of living, as prior to rights of property. Judaism emphasizes the duty of charity, and strives for a social

order which will protect men against the material disabilities of old age, sickness and unemployment.

8. *Peace.* Judaism, from the days of the prophets, has proclaimed to mankind the ideal of universal peace. The spiritual and physical disarmament of all nations has been one of its essential teachings. It abhors all violence and relies upon moral education, love and sympathy to secure human progress. It regards justice as the foundation of the well-being of nations and the condition of enduring peace. It urges organized international action for disarmament, collective security and world peace.

III. RELIGIOUS PRACTICE

9. *The Religious Life.* Jewish life is marked by consecration to these ideals of Judaism. It calls for faithful participation in the life of the Jewish community as it finds expression in home, synagog and school and in all other agencies that enrich Jewish life and promote its welfare.

The *Home* has been and must continue to be a stronghold of Jewish life, hallowed by the spirit of love and reverence, by moral discipline and religious observance and worship.

The *Synagog* is the oldest and most democratic institution in Jewish life. It is the prime communal agency by which Judaism is fostered and preserved. It links the Jews of each community and unites them with all Israel.

The perpetuation of Judaism as a living force depends upon religious knowledge and upon the *Education* of each new generation in our rich cultural and spiritual heritage.

Prayer is the voice of religion, the language of faith and aspiration. It directs man's heart and mind Godward, voices the needs and hopes of the community, and reaches out after goals which invest life with supreme value. To deepen the spiritual life of our people, we must cultivate the traditional habit of communion with God through prayer in both home and synagog.

Judaism as *a way of life* requires in addition to its moral and spiritual demands, the preservation of the Sabbath, festivals and Holy Days, the retention and development of such customs, symbols and ceremonies as possess inspirational value, the cultivation of distinctive forms of religious art and music and the use of Hebrew, together with the vernacular, in our worship and instruction.

These timeless aims and ideals of our faith we present anew to a confused and troubled world. We call upon our fellow Jews to rededicate themselves to them, and, in harmony with all men, hopefully and courageously to continue Israel's eternal quest after God and His kingdom.

We have looked at a number of the most crucial statements of Jewish belief. On the one hand, they seem to imply that Judaism does stand for something specific. They disagree on many details, but all of them assert that there is a God and that to believe in God means Jews must believe in some other truths also. If there is a God, all of these writers imply, then other truths follow from His existence, even though we disagree about just which truths or how many of them. So Jews do seem to believe something in common, and this agreement implies a kind of necessity to believe.

But that is not the same thing as a "creed." It is not something forced upon you from outside yourself. It is not on idea you must accept nor a statement you must speak in order to join Judaism. It is not a belief which will guarantee your getting into Heaven or staying out of mischief. There is no Jewish creed like that of some religions without which one cannot belong to the faith nor expect its reward. As Abba Hillel Silver, a leading liberal Rabbi of our own time, tells us:

> Faith (*Emunah*) in Judaism . . . is not creed or belief in the accepted usage of these terms. It is rather stead-

fastness to a course prescribed, firm and zealous adherence
to a code of moral practice revealed to man, and confidence in the right outcome of all things willed by God
and of all action acceptable to Him. *Emunah* derives from
the same root as *Aman,* master workman—it is inseparable
from action.

Faith is not believing a creed so much as it is stick-
ing to a path. It is not so much saying what God is or
even that He is, as it is trusting Him in one's own life.
Leo Baeck, the greatest Rabbi of the twentieth century,
whose faith was tested in the concentration camps, insists that Jewish faith is different from other religions'.
It is not something forced upon us which makes us
obey. Belief is, rather, a plan by which the Jew moves
toward God:

> Man becomes a believer when he experiences himself
> in the direction of God, and directs himself toward God
> in such a way that no part of his life can be without this
> center, and without this contact. Thus his heart becomes
> unified as an old prayer expresses it—united in the One
> God.
> Faith is therefore no commanded faith. "Thou shalt be-
> lieve" would be an alien commandment; faith is ordering.
> Faith is not a requested acceptance of a truth, nor
> seizure by an overwhelming feeling, neither orthodoxy
> nor mystic ecstasy but the choice of a starting point and of
> a way. Faith is expressed neither by emotions nor by
> theories but by a decision.
> It is not a confession of God's existence but a will for
> God. Faith is an all-embracing will toward the One
> within and above the earthly, within the world as well as
> beyond the world, a will toward that which is more than
> appears.

Faith, as Baeck says, is not an act of the mind which
agrees to a proposition. It is not an act of the emotions

which feels a sensation. It is not an act of the mouth which states something. It is rather a direction of the whole person, a life lived toward God.

The creedal statements we have considered do not force us into anything. They only show us where our fathers and their fathers have stood. Judaism is not just whatever you or I believe this year; it is also what a hundred generations have believed before us. Sometimes we agree with those who preceded us, sometimes we cannot or will not. But we still are Jews.

We are not told to "accept" any creed, not even the principles of Maimonides or the Columbus Platform. Judaism tells us to search on our own. Judaism is walking within the paths our fathers walked, and sometimes a step or two outside. The Baal Shem Tov, the great leader of Hasidism in Europe two hundred years ago, insisted that the very essence of Jewish belief is not only continuity but change:

> Why do we pray: "Our God and God of our fathers?" There are two sorts of persons who believe in God. The one believes because his faith has been handed down to him by his fathers; and his faith is strong. The other has arrived at faith by searching thought. And this is the difference between the two: The first has the advantage that his faith cannot be shaken, no matter how many objections are raised to it, for his faith is firm because he has taken it over from his fathers. But there is a flaw in it; it is a commandment given by man, and it has been learned without thought or reasoning. The advantage of the second man is that he has reached faith through his own power, through much searching and thinking. His faith too has a flaw; it is easy to shake it by offering contrary evidence. But he who combines both kinds of faith

is invulnerable. That is why we say: "Our God," because of our searching, and "the God of our fathers," because of our tradition.

And a similar interpretation holds when we say, "The God of Abraham, the God of Isaac, and the God of Jacob," for this means: Isaac and Jacob did not merely take over the tradition of Abraham, but sought out the divine for themselves.

If it was true in eighteenth century Orthodoxy that each Jew had to seek God for himself, it is more obviously so today. Perhaps more clearly than ever before, we cannot pick up where the older thinkers left off. This is a time for new ways of thinking, new questions, new directions to search. We must begin with the world in which *we* live, a world of atomic science and psychoanalysis and outer space probes. The questions that we ask must be asked in a new way. But we can still ask them of the old Judaism. Our task is to inquire with firmness and honesty, holding nothing back, beginning inevitably with our own world. But we must ask all the great masters of Jewish thought and listen patiently to their response. Together we shall inspect what Jewish teachers of many generations have thought. But we shall hear them as possible replies to our own present-day questions.

For better or worse, Judaism now depends not on them but on us. All the thought and passion and search since the time of the Bible are now put into our hands. As Abraham Joshua Heschel, a leading present-day Jewish thinker, writes, it is up to us either to fulfill our history or to betray it:

The moment at Sinai depends for its fulfillment upon this present moment, upon all moments. Had Israel been disloyal subsequent to Sinai, that great moment would have been deprived of all meaning. The Tablets are broken whenever the golden calf is called into being. We believe that every hour is endowed with the power to lend meaning to—or withhold meaning from—all other hours.

The responsibility of creating Judaism's future may seem to you too great. You may be troubled by your own uncertainties and doubts. You may be concerned by the contradictory answers which this chapter has offered. You will be more troubled as contradictions multiply in succeeding pages. But Judaism, since it is for human beings, inevitably involves uncertainty and contradiction. There is no party-line in Judaism. There is no saving dogma. There is no simple solution. There is only a way to go, questions to ponder, and a God to share your search.

The Talmud records that the great schools of Hillel and Shammai almost always disagreed. When once they did, a heavenly voice said: "These and these are the words of the Living God." This is usually thought to mean that one school was right and the other, though contradictory, was somehow right too. But it may mean that "these *and* these"—only both together—are the words of God. Only when Hillel and Shammai, the contradictory authorities, are set forth together can we hope to find God. Maimonides and Kohler and Baeck do not agree entirely, but we need all of them. No one source, not even the Bible, can give us ready-made answers. The rabbis showed they understood that truth, by commenting on the Bible in hundreds of different ways. The purpose of this book is not to solve all the riddles, but to point out landmarks and to encourage deeper search.

Why should we try to answer these difficult questions? If the rabbis and the philosophers could not agree, why should we open the issues again? Why should you read these chapters if you can be sure in advance they will fail? Why should you come to this book hoping it will do what far greater books could not do?

The book of Deuteronomy commands that we go to a "judge that shall be in those days." And on this verse the Talmud makes a striking comment:

> The Torah commands: "Thou shalt come unto the priests, the Levites, and unto the judge that shall be in those days." Could it possibly enter your mind that a person would go to a judge who was *not* in his days! The meaning is, "You are to go only to a living authority."

The reason this book may help you search is that it is trying to put living questions that are real for living Jews, especially younger Jews. We want to see what Judaism has to say to you. You will have to decide for yourself whether Judaism is worth what it costs in decision and obedience, in originality and in study. There is no creed to do your work for you.

And you, too, will fail. You will never complete the search. You will never find *the* answer. Your faith will always be struggle. The Talmud quotes God as saying, "Would they had abandoned Me and kept my Torah."

To the Baal Shem Tov this meant that God wanted us to seek for Him even if we know the limits of our own search, to try to wrest the secrets from His world, even though we cannot wholly succeed.

> "Had they but abandoned Me," says God, "and kept faith with My Torah!"
>
> This must be interpreted as follows: The end of knowledge is to know that we cannot know anything. But there are two sorts of not-knowing. The one is immediate not-knowing, when a man does not even begin to examine and try to know, because it is impossible to know. Another, however, examines and seeks, until he comes to know that one cannot know. And the difference between these two—to whom may we compare them? To two men who wish to see the king. The one enters all the chambers belonging to the king. He rejoices in the king's treasure rooms and splendid halls, and then he discovers that he cannot get to know the king. The other tells himself: "Since it is not possible to get to know the king, we will not bother to enter, but put up with not knowing."
>
> This leads us to understand what those words of God mean. They have abandoned Me, that is, they have abandoned the search to know Me, because it is not possible. But oh, I wish they "abandoned" Me with searching and understanding, so keeping faith with My Torah!

Welcome to a road that has no end!

CHAPTER TWO

Is There a God?

IF YOU can prove there is a God, why doesn't everyone believe in Him? If you can't, why do so many people in the world today, and the vast majority of those who ever lived, believe He exists?

These are the two sides of the problem of God's existence with which some of us wrestle all our lives. There is too much evidence that He exists to dismiss God from our accounting. But there doesn't seem to be the kind of proof for His existence that compels our belief. Nearly everyone believes in God (or used to), but no one can explain his belief so forcefully that anyone who hears his explanation must agree.

The Bible knew that some people didn't believe in God. We know this from the first verse of a Psalm (it comes twice in the Bible, as number fourteen and again as number fifty-three). The Psalm may be translated accurately, if not elegantly:

"The square said to himself: 'There is no God.' "

The Bible knows of the person who isn't convinced there is a God, but it calls him a *novol* which means someone who is both stupid and blind. This "square" just doesn't see what there is to see; he just doesn't "dig" the world. Not only that, but because he is blind, he is likely to act blindly. He knows nothing, so he is likely to do everything wrong. He is so far "out," that he is virtually certain to be wicked. He is so unperceptive that he cannot be trusted. That is why he says there is no God. Because he is too blind to see God all around him, or too selfish to share his own world with the Creator of it. At least, that is what the Bible seems to think.

The Bible knows about the atheist, the man who says there is no God. But the Biblical writers do not waste time trying to convince him he is wrong. They consider the atheist a fool who is too dull to understand or too wicked to let himself be convinced.

So you will not find anywhere in the Bible an argument for the existence of God. In virtually all of Judaism, the existence of God is assumed. It is rarely proved. It is the root of the Jewish religion, not its fruit. It is the beginning, not the end, of our search. Speaking of the post-Biblical teachers, Rabbi Abba Hillel Silver says they:

> began with God and the Torah and they never wandered any distance away from them. The author of the *Letter of Aristeas* noted: "For in their conduct and discourse these men (the Sages who were sent from Palestine

to Alexandria to translate the Bible into Greek) were far in advance of the philosophers, for they made their starting-point from God."

The Jewish philosopher Philo, who lived about the time of Jesus, agrees. He knows, there are some people who are not convinced that there is a God, but he thinks, these are "wicked men (who) hide from God." Philo divides all men into two groups: one group knows that God is the center and meaning of all things. The other denies God because it trusts in human power and in the human mind as master of all. But Philo doesn't try to convert the unbeliever. He simply warns people to choose God and not to put their ultimate confidence in human resources.

> He who flees from God, flees into himself. For there are two kinds of mind—the mind of the universe, and that is God—and the mind of the individual man. And the one who flees from his own mind to the mind of the universe—for whoever leaves his own mind, avows therewith that the works of the mortal mind are as nothing, and ascribes everything to God. But the other flees from God, and declares that not God is the cause of anything at all, but that he himself is the cause of all that comes to pass. Thus there are many who believe that all the things in the world go their own course by themselves, without a guide, and that it is the spirit of man that has invented the arts, crafts, laws, customs, state institutions, and the rights of the individual and the community. But you, oh my soul, see the difference between these two points of view. For the one leaves the perishable mortal mind, which has been created, and chooses for its true aid the immortal mind of the universe. But the other, which sets aside God, foolishly courts as its ally the human mind, which is not even able to help itself.

This plea of Philo's may well leave us cold. We are not so ready to put people into two absolute categories. We would not set the spirit of man against the belief in God. We ourselves sometimes rely on our own mind, sometimes on the "Mind of the universe." We may well believe that God uses man to change the world. In any case, our world does not divide itself into atheists and believers quite that neatly.

Most Jews of the past, however, never really considered the possibility that there is no God. Even when they met atheistic people or cynical philosophers, they never really admitted that maybe there is no God. They did not often ask whether or not He existed, but only what He was like, and what He wanted them to do. If someone denied God, he was to them as silly as someone who denies that two and two make four is to us.

But for us there is no such certainty. We cannot call all atheists fools. We sometimes feel God's existence with a deep certainty, but often we ourselves are not so sure, and sometimes we may be tempted to deny Him altogether.

Even the Biblical writers understood that God was not always close to man. They knew that (as Jeremiah said) He is a God "far off" who sometimes "hides Himself." They meant that God always exists, but sometimes it is really hard for man to find Him. Sometimes, they told us, men hide from God as Adam did. Sometimes God seems to hide from man, too. A beautiful tale of the Hasidim, the pious European Jews of sev-

eral centuries ago, reminds us that it is not just the
very wicked or the very stupid who cannot find God.

> Rabbi Barukh's grandson Yehiel was once playing
> hide-and-seek with another boy. He hid himself well and
> waited for his playmate to find him. When he had waited
> for a long time, he came out of his hiding-place, but the
> other was nowhere to be seen; now Yehiel realized that
> he had not looked for him from the very beginning. This
> made him cry, and crying he ran to his grandfather and
> complained of his faithless friend. Then tears brimmed
> in Rabbi Barukh's eyes and he said, "God says the same
> thing: 'I hide but no one wants to seek me.'"

The Bible sees, then, that man is not always sure of
God. We know that all too well. We cannot find God
every time we look. And sometimes we do not even
look. We cannot simply assume the existence of God
as many of our forefathers did. We have to see whether
or not we are convinced by the evidence.

It is very important whether or not there is a God.
Some questions make very little difference. Some puz-
zles are irrelevant to our life and it doesn't count
whether we figure them out or not. But some issues are
important to mankind. Of these, too, some may be very
important, but not to us personally (like mathematical
questions)—and only a very few are of the highest importance to every one of us. It is of these questions
that Franz Rosenzweig, the great German-Jewish
teacher of the early part of our century, wrote:

> From those unimportant truths of the type "twice two
> equal four," to which men lightly assent with the expendi-
> ture of no more than a trifle mind energy—a little less
> for the ordinary multiplication table, a little more for the
> theory of relativity—the way leads to the truths for which

a man is willing to pay something, on to those which he cannot prove true except with the sacrifice of his life, and finally to those the truth of which can be proved only by staking the lives of all the generations.

Jews have given much for the belief in God's existence. The generations of Jews have staked everything that He exists. They have sacrificed, lived, and given up their lives for the "sanctification of God's name," to show mankind that He is. And decision for or against God is still necessary. We must make up our own minds whether or not there is a God, because our lives will be different with Him than without. As Abraham Heschel, a great teacher of our own time, insists, we cannot suspend judgment.

> Man cannot afford to be noncommital about a reality upon which the meaning and manner of his existence depend. He is driven toward some sort of affirmation. In whatever decision he makes, he implicitly accepts either the presence of God or the absurdity of denying it. The nonsense of denial is too monstrous to be conceivable, since it implies that the universe is all alone except for the company of man, that the mind of man surpasses everything within and beyond the universe.

We live with God or without, not somewhere suspended between. We may live sometimes as if He exists, and sometimes not, but in any case, our opinion has real consequences. Maimonides, the greatest Jewish philosopher of all, believed that to one who truly knows God nothing else really counts. Only God's presence is ultimately important.

> It is well known and quite evident that the love of God cannot strike deep root in the heart of man unless

it occupies his mind constantly, so that nothing in the world matters to him but this love of God.

We must decide whether God is. If He exists, then there are a great many tasks which follow for us. If not, we must learn to live in a world empty except for men. Why then do people believe there is a God? There are three kinds of reasons for believing that there is a God. One comes from the world in which we live. One grows from the interpretation of the world found in the Torah. And the third comes out of our own experience in the world. The first of these is from nature, the second from Scripture, the third from experience.

Nature points to God. That is the view of many Biblical and later Jewish writers. The author of the nineteenth psalm looked out on the world, looked up to the sky and felt certain there is a God.

> The heavens declare the glorious existence of God and the sky tells that He made it.

The author of the fortieth chapter of the book of Isaiah invites us to:

> Lift up your eyes and see Who created these things, the One Who brings the group of them by number, Who calls them all by name.

God, according to the Biblical writers, is found when we look up, when we *really* look up. God is not in the sky, but the sky shows that He made it. God is not among the stars, but the stars are obviously His work. The universe points to God. It moves in regular order, so He must have ordered it. It is there, so He must have brought it into being. It is beautiful, so a Divine Artist must have etched it. It changes and grows and decays, so One who does not change must make it able to continue.

Some of these are conclusions about nature that the Bible does not draw specifically, but in many passages like the ones we quoted, the Bible believes the world shows God. Remember that the Bible is not really interested in proving His bare existence. Man's choice, according to the Bible, is not *whether* he will believe in God or not, but *which* god he will choose. Man must have his god, but will it be the Creator of the universe or a little idol? The Bible is not concerned with the danger of atheism but of idolatry. And it tries to argue from the world we see to the true God who is not part of it but brought it into being. The Bible is not interested in proving that there is a God, but that the God who is, is really a Creator and a King.

However, does the world really give us an unmistakable proof for God's existence? Do the heavens declare His existence to everyone? There is order in nature, of course, but there is also disorder. There is beauty, to be sure, but there is also ugliness. The world is only able to manifest God to certain kinds of men. Not everyone will go from the natural world to the Creator.

The Bible knows that, too. The very psalm which asserts that the heavens show forth God, continues:

> The Torah of God is whole, turning the soul.
> The witness of God is trustworthy, making the simple man wise.

> The statutes of God are straightforward, making the
> heart glad.
> The commandment of God is pure, enlightening the eyes.

Why does the Psalmist move from Nature to the
Torah, from God in the world to God in the Bible?
Because here is another, perhaps a more compelling
reason for following the road to the true God. The
heavens show Him; so, even more clearly, does Torah.

Does not the Torah say it came from God? "Thus
saith God," "And the Lord spoke," "The word of the
Lord came." Does not the Bible claim to tell us, not
only that there is a God, but that He wants certain
things and feels certain emotions and loves and creates?
If we believe the Torah, then it proves there is a God.

But do we believe the Torah? Certainly, the liberal
Jew and the Orthodox Jew differ on what Torah
means. We shall discuss this problem in a chapter of
its own. But, in any case, the disagreement is not over
what Torah means about God; Torah is central in
liberal Judaism, too, and therefore it is an impressive
witness to the Giver of the Torah. The commandment
implies a Commander-in-Chief. The Word points to a
Giver of the Torah. Kaufmann Kohler, one of the
earliest leaders of American Reform Judaism, wrote:

> Reason alone will not lead to God, except where reli-
> gious intuition forms, so to speak, the ladder of heaven,
> leading to the realm of the unknowable. Philosophy, at
> best, can only demonstrate the existence of a final Cause,
> or of a supreme Intelligence working toward sublime pur-
> poses; possibly also a moral government of the world, in
> both the physical and the spiritual life. Religion alone,
> founded upon divine revelation, can teach man to find

a God, to whom he can appeal in trust in his moments of trouble or of woe, and whose will he can see in the dictates of conscience and the destiny of nations.

But do we not seem to be going in a circle? How do I know there is a God? Because the Torah tells me so. How do I know the Torah is telling the truth? Because God gave it. How can religion found its belief in God on "divine revelation," when the source of that revelation is the same God it tries to prove? If religion alone can prove there is a God, how can the non-believer ever find Him? How can the Bible show us God, when it itself is a problem for us? The Orthodox Jew has no problem with Torah. It is the unquestioned guide of his life. And so, for him, God is no problem either because the Torah says He exists.

For us liberal Jews the Torah is full of problems. Yet somehow the fact that they are *our* problems shows us that the Torah brings something important to us. If we didn't think Torah was important, we wouldn't worry about the many problems in Bible and Tradition. When we read the Torah, however, we find that God is everywhere in it. The experience of Bible men and the writings they left us seem to say that God moved through their lives, inspired their beliefs, changed them. If that is true, there must be a God. But though the Bible may teach us in this way to have faith in God, we do not have faith in the Bible as God. We do not believe that any single sentence or single book proves there is a God. But the greatness and mystery of Biblical man's experience points toward the greatness and mystery of God.

The Bible is full of stories of how men found God or how God found them. Adam discovers God in his own growing-up, even in his own failures. Abraham hears a command to go out to a land he never saw to serve a God neither he nor any man will ever see. Jacob wrestles all night with a man, but when at last dawn comes, he says, "I have seen God face to face and am alive." Moses, wandering in the desert far from where his true task lies, sees a bush lit up like a neon sign, and Moses believes he is in the presence of God. Isaiah catches a glimpse of God in the Temple, but it is a God Whom no Temple can contain. Job, in agony and ashes, seeks God where many suffering men finally have found him. The Psalmists, in ecstasy and fear and joy, are made so certain there is a God that they forget to tell us how they know. But they do know.

In these books, in this Torah, we have a sign-post pointing Godward. Like the natural world, the world of Scripture is holy. And it is holy because it is more than only natural, more than simply human. But the Torah will not put God in our pocket. It will not "prove" that He exists, as a scientific book proves theorems. It will offer nothing to a man who reads it with suspicion or hatred. It is only valuable to one who opens himself to its music. Jewish faith is not accepting a truth; it is being ready for a mystery. It is not accepting proof; it is awaiting experience. As Martin Buber, one of the greatest thinkers of our own time, says:

> Real faith does not mean professing what we hold true in a ready-made formula. On the contrary: it means holding ourselves open to the unconditioned mystery which

we encounter in every sphere of our life and which cannot be comprised in any formula. It means that, from the very roots of our being, we should always be prepared to live with this mystery as one being lives with another.

So the idea of God that comes from the natural world and the idea of God that comes from our Jewish history and literature reach toward a single point. That point is you. The Torah is not just a book we read or a tradition we study. It is a direction for living people. It is a part of your life. This is the decisive "proof." God is to be found in your own life, or you will not find Him at all. Claude Montefiore, the English Jewish liberal of a generation ago, put it this way:

> The religion of a man is not, in the truest sense of the word, something outside him or something which he has "learnt" but it is part of himself, it is a part of his own feelings, convictions, experience. We do not know God in the same sense as we know that the leaves of a tree are green, or that two and two make four, but yet we may fairly speak of a knowledge of God, so far as God answers to our deepest moral needs, so far as we "realize" him in prayer, so far as we cannot explain the world or ourselves without him, so far as we are inwardly convinced of his existence and his influence.

The experience of God may be dramatic or almost invisible. It may be sudden or painfully slow. But it is in personal experience that the world of nature and tradition become ways of reaching God.

Perhaps you have had such an experience of the Divine. It may have been in seeing one of the great beauties of the natural world when an unforgettable sunset or a peaceful stream made you think of nature in a new and different way. It may have been reading the Bible or a synagogue service, perhaps on a holy day, when the words came to life and answered your question to God. Thus Nature or Tradition were, for you at least, proof of God.

Or, perhaps, it may have been in the love of your family or friend that God's love seemed to be very near and very precious. It may have been when you won a victory or fell very ill that God made His presence known to you. It may have been an unexpected visit, or one you hoped for very long. You may have had a vision of Him, or simply a long and painful search. But you have had these experiences, or will, or can. Those who seek God with all their heart have, somehow, seemed to find Him. And they prove to all of us that He is there to seek.

Some men have found God in their struggle with good and evil. It is very hard to be good in our world, and yet sometimes we do achieve goodness and feel Someone who is good is helping us. In the whole struggle to overcome war and injustice, when we take part in the struggle, we learn that man is not absolutely alone. In our own lives, when we choose the mature over the immature, the longer-range need over the short-run pleasure, we feel a holy companionship. Even when we fall short, we often experience a sense of forgiveness that seems Divine. If good is really to survive and conquer evil in the world, it must be because there is One both very powerful and very good Who helps us. Ethical experience, too, leads to God.

In fact, the whole idea that our world makes sense,

leads us to believe in God. If the world is no accident, but a meaningful arena of human struggle and accomplishment, then God must have made it so. If our own personal lives move from broken confusion to an ever-growing wholeness and significance, then we are part of a creation. Even our failures show that there is a standard beyond the human standard. Our small successes make us humble enough to admit that He is here, too.

The Hasidim tell many stories about people who did not believe in God until a great teacher showed them how. One of their most perceptive tales shows how simple and yet how mysterious is the turning of man's heart.

A very learned man who had heard of the rabbi of Berditchev—one of those who boasted of being enlightened—looked him up in order to debate with him as he was in the habit of doing with others, and refuting his old-fashioned proofs for the truth of his faith. When he entered the zaddik's (Holy teacher's) room, he saw him walking up and down, a book in his hand, immersed in ecstatic thought. The rabbi took no notice of his visitor. After a time, however, he stopped, gave him a brief glance and said: "But perhaps it is true after all!" In vain did the learned man try to rally his self-confidence. His knees shook, for the zaddik was terrible to behold and his simple words were terrible to hear. But now Rabbi Levi Yitzhak turned to him and calmly addressed him: "My son, the great Torah scholars with whom you debated, wasted their words on you. When you left them you only laughed at what they had said. They could not set God and his kingdom on the table before you, and I cannot do this either. But, my son, only think! Perhaps it is true.

Perhaps it is true after all!" The enlightened man made the utmost effort to reply, but the terrible "perhaps" beat on his ears again and again and broke down his resistance.

For those of us who want reasons, there are many for believing in God. Some of these are metaphysical; they come from an analysis of the world. Some are ethical; they come from understanding our own personal lives and our effort to do good. Some are historical; they come from the record of mankind, and especially from the sacred tradition of the Jewish people. Rabbi Milton Steinberg has summarized these arguments for the existence of God.

1. There are arguments metaphysical:
   —The argument from design, that the nature of Nature and the endowments of man are inexplicable except through God;
   —The argument from causation, that an existent universe is proof of a cause at least equal to itself;
2. There are arguments ethical:
   —The argument from man's emotional and moral needs, that without a God to give meaning to things and sanction to ideals, human existence is pointless, aspirations are delusions, and life is devoid of purpose and hope;
   —The argument from the experiences of men and nations, that only the good is stable while evil tends to destroy itself—a circumstance indicative of an ethical power as the motivating force behind the universe.
3. There are arguments historical:
   —The arguments based on the careers of peoples; and arguments mystical centering about the persistent reports—brought by some souls in each generation—of inner illuminations resulting from direct contact, outside thought and the senses, with Deity.

And first, last, and all the time, there are the arguments resting on revelation, prophecy, and miracle as recorded in Scripture and the Tradition.

Some people will be and have been convinced by these arguments. For them, the existence of God is as sure as their own existence which also cannot be "proved." Some people remain unconvinced. Perhaps they are not convinced because they have not thought about it long enough or hard enough. It is a fact of religion that only those who search for God may find Him. Perhaps personal tragedy or blindness obscures God from some eyes. Perhaps some people wish there would be no God.

To the man who does not seek God, the endless and always incomplete aspiration of the seeker may seem foolish. But the religious man has no choice but to continue looking for God. And he knows why the unbeliever cannot or will not share his search.

> Rabbi Moshe Hayyim Efraim, the Baal Shem's grandson, told: "I heard this from my grandfather: Once a fiddler played so sweetly that all who heard him began to dance, and whoever came near enough to hear, joined in the dance. Then a deaf man who knew nothing of music, happened along, and to him all he saw seemed the action of madmen—senseless and in bad taste."

CHAPTER THREE

What Is God Like?

No one can ever know exactly what God is like. "If I knew God, I would be God," says the Hebrew poet. The Talmud lists four problems about which a man should not trouble to think. They are "hidden"; they are beyond our power to know.

> Whosoever gives his mind to four things, it were better for him if he had not come into the world: What is above? What is beneath? What was beforetime? And what will be hereafter? What is too wonderful for you, do not seek, nor search after what is hidden from you. Meditate upon that which is permitted to you. Do not occupy yourself with mysteries.

If we cannot know "what is above," then we cannot ever wholly grasp God; no matter how hard we try, He is too far above us. His ways, as Isaiah says, are not our ways, "for as the Heaven is high above the earth," so is He far above our powers to find out. Sometimes the ancient Greeks and Romans, who pushed the human mind to its farthest extremes, insisted on knowing just what God is like. When they did, they got into trouble. They were seeking the impossible, and their search was doomed.

> It is recorded that the emperor Hadrian said to Joshua ben Hananya: "I desire to behold your God." "That is an impossibility," he replied. The emperor persisted; so the Rabbi bade him face the sun, it being the time of the summer solstice, and said: "Gaze at that." "I cannot," he answered. Whereupon the Rabbi exclaimed: "You admit that you are unable to look at the sun, which is only one of the attendants upon the Holy One, blessed be He; how much more beyond your power must it be to look at God Himself!"

But even if we cannot look on God Himself, and it is important to remember that we cannot, no matter how much we should like to, it may yet be that God has told us something of Himself. It may be that we can know, not all God is, but all we can know about all God is. And that insight which is not everything may be something. If we can know anything at all, that knowledge would be very precious.

The Bible tells us that when God called Moses at the burning bush, Moses asked His name. Now a "name" in the Biblical writings is more than just something to call someone. A name is an essence; it means what someone really is. The Name of God is a brief answer to the question: What is God like?

Even today sometimes a name means something essential. A woman who gets married changes her name to show that she is a new person with a new role. A nickname may mean something about the nature of a person. "Lefty" probably bats left-handed. "Ginger" is likely to be a sharp and peppery kind of girl. But Moses' question asked for the Name of God. He wanted to know as much about God's real being as he could.

According to the book of Exodus, God answered him with the name we read *Adonoi,* and said it means: "I shall be what I shall be." That is not a very illuminating answer at first sight. As we might have expected, God's name is much more elusive and complicated than Lefty's. God is much harder to know or to talk about than any human being who ever lived.

"I shall be" seems to mean that God is the One who is. He really is. He always will be. And He always will be for us, with us. He wanted Moses to tell the slaves in Egypt that God still lived, and that He was with them. He wanted to tell mankind that He lives, and that He will always be there to help us when we need Him. But, he said, "I shall be *what I shall be.*" That means that God who will be, will be what He is, in the way and as the One Who He is. He will come to be with the people in Egypt, but not necessarily in the way they wish, or at the time they wish, or to do just what they want. He will deliver them from Egypt, as they hope, but He will bring them to a new place and a new destiny, as He wishes. He will always be. But He will not be with us simply to do what we want Him to do. He can always be found by men, but not in the way they select or in the appearance they expect. He will be as *He* will be.

What the Bible tells us about God here and elsewhere is less than we wish to know about Him. It is also less than the Biblical men knew about Him. A newspaper may report a child's birth, but his parents know that something more than the newspaper tells has happened. The Department of Defense informs a mother that her son is killed in action, but she experiences much more than they can tell. She cannot communicate all she knows about her lost son, but she surely knows more than the government does. So, too, a religious man, like the author of Exodus, knows more about God than he can tell. But he does tell us that, somehow, God can be known. We shall see what the knowledge hinted in the answer to Moses means.

There is an immediate problem in talking about God. As the Mekilta, a rabbinic commentary on the Book of Exodus, tells us: "We borrow terms from His creatures to apply to Him in order to help us understand." All that we say about God must be said in human speech. Our speech is imperfect and cannot fully apply to God. It is designed to describe creatures, and God is not a created thing. Our best attempts fail, yet our words may enclose a kernel of real knowledge.

We seem always to talk about God as if He were a man. But we know He is not a man, or He could not be God. To "help us understand," we use the only language we have. But it is not good enough to describe God even insofar as we can come to know Him. The danger of using human analogy to talk about God is called "anthropomorphism." It makes the mistake of talking as if God were no more than we are. But as the Talmud says:

> The Holy One, blessed be He, said: "I am the first, for I have no father. I am the last, for I have no brother. Beside me there is no God, for I have no son."

We all have parents. All of us parents have children. But God is not at all like us, for He is God. The great Jewish philosopher, Maimonides, had no patience with those Jews who held on to anthropomorphic, humanizing ideas of God:

> If you think that there is an excuse for those who believe that God has a body on the ground of their training, their ignorance, or their weak understanding, you must make the same concession to the worshipper of idols. You may say that the literal interpretation of the Bible causes men to fall into that doubt, but you must know that idolaters were also brought to their belief by false ideas. There is no excuse for those who, if they are unable to think it out for themselves, do not accept the teaching of the non-human nature of God from true philosophers.

This, then, is our first problem. Human speech is designed to talk about human things. But God is not a human being. All of us, as soon as we say anything about God, approach the error of anthropomorphism. But we cannot help ourselves. The Bible often talks of God in human terms. None of us can avoid the danger. Kaufmann Kohler, a leader of American Reform Judaism, reminds us of the inevitable mistake:

> . . . we must bear in mind that we naturally ascribe to God a human personality, whether we speak of Him as the Master-worker of the universe, as the all-seeing and all-hearing Judge, or the compassionate and merciful Father. We cannot help attributing human qualities and emotions to Him the moment we invest Him with a moral and spiritual nature. When we speak of His puni-

tive justice, His unfailing mercy, or His all-wise providence, we transfer to Him, imperceptibly, our own righteous indignation at the sight of a wicked deed, or our
own compassion with the sufferer, or even our own mode
of deliberation and decision. Moreover, the prophets and
the Torah, in order to make God plain to the people,
described Him in vivid images of human life, with anger
and jealousy as well as compassion and repentance, and
also with the organs and functions of the senses—seeing,
hearing, smelling, speaking, and walking. The rabbis are
all the more emphatic in their assertions that the Torah
merely intends to assist the simple-minded, and that un-
seemly expressions concerning Deity are due to the in-
adequacy of language, and must not be taken literally.

We talk about God in human terms, because we are
human beings and have no other way. But perhaps we
use these terms, also, because we feel God is not entirely different from us, but in some way, like us. We
seem to believe that He is not wholly different from
us and absolutely unknowable, but, in some measure,
near and known. The rabbis say that the false idols of
other men "act like strangers toward those who worship them." But we do not consider our God a stranger.
We talk of Him in human terms partly because we feel
He is something like the human persons we love.
Claude Montefiore writes:

God is not *only* unlike man. There *is* a kinship between
them, a *delegated* kinship, with which God has endowed
us. By delegated, I mean that this kinship comes from,
and is given us, by God. The spirit through which we ac-
quire knowledge and goodness, through which we love
knowledge and goodness, and will to do good and loving
deeds, is of divine origin: it is, as some would say, God
in us, the divine spirit in us—that divine spirit of holiness
which the Psalmist prayed to God that he should not

42

take away from him. Our knowledge has been achieved—
it has been possible for us to achieve it—and it is a true
knowledge, so far as it has gone or can go, because our
reason is akin to the reason of God. Our goodness has
been achieved—it is a real and true goodness, so far as
it goes or can go, because it is not wholly unlike, or alien
to, the goodness of God.

The God of the Bible is not a human being. He is,
as we shall see, mysterious and hidden in obscurity.
But He is also a near God, not wholly unlike the man
He made in His image. God is not just like any human
being we happen to know, not even the best one. But
He is more like what we call a person than like anything else we know. When we consider what we believe
about God, that He loves and teaches and helps, we
are talking about someone who is more like our best
friend than He is like the moon or the second law of
thermo-dynamics. We use human speech in talking
about God, then, not only because we must, but also
because it is not wholly unusable. Rabbi Leo Baeck
reminds us that Jews have had many different notions
of God. But the one thread that runs through them all
is that He is like a Person, though not a human one
in all its imperfections. God is like a Person who cares
about us and makes demands of us.

The personal God is the God of trust, but not the god
of a system, nor a mere idea of God. The Jewish people
clung to this personal God. It spoke to Him in the most
intimate way, even when it only called Him "The Name."
Freedom of thought was always granted to the people;
nothing limited searching thought, nor the longing for
an even truer expression. A philosophy (of God) both
rational and mystic developed, intense and diverse at the

same time. But one thing was always firmly established: the one and personal God, the "I am Who I am," the One who said: "I am He Who is Your God: You must . . ."

You may remember from the prayer book, the best source of what Jews have thought about God through the centuries, these words. They remind us that God is not absolutely other than we are, that He sometimes comes very close to us:

> Blessed be Thou, gracious giver of knowledge.
> Blessed be Thou, who desirest repentance.
> Blessed be Thou, who abundantly forgives.
> Blessed be Thou, who lovest righteousness and justice.
> Blessed be Thou, who healest the sick.
> Blessed be Thou, who hearest prayer.

If God can give knowledge, heal the sick, hear prayer, then He is very like us. We may not agree with the author of this prayer that God acts in so literal or immediate a way, but we still pray to a God who in some way hears us and cares. The very existence of Jewish prayer proves that Jews think of God as one who is near us and loves us. The fact that we call him "Thou," or "You," means that we think He can be reached and, if not wholly understood, still loved. The Talmud sharply contrasts the Jewish God, who is not far away from man, with the strange gods of the ancient peoples.

> A ship, belonging to a heathen owner, was once sailing over the sea, one of the passengers being a Jewish boy. A great storm arose, and all the Gentiles aboard took hold of their idols and prayed to them, but to no avail. Seeing that their prayers had been in vain, they said to the lad: "Call upon your God, for we have heard that He answers your petitions when you cry to Him and that He

is all-powerful." The boy immediately stood up and called with his heart upon God, Who hearkened to his prayer, and the sea became calm. On reaching land, they disembarked to purchase their requirements and said to him: "Do you not wish to buy anything?" He answered: "What do you want of a poor alien like me?" They exclaimed: "You a poor alien! We are the poor aliens; for some of us are here and have our gods in Babylon; others have them in Rome; others have their gods with them but they are of no benefit to us. As for you, however, wherever you go your God is with you!"

The pagans were "aliens" because their gods were silent and unapproachable. Their gods were things or ideas or forces. But the Jewish God always has seemed to be concerned and universally present.

We are very much afraid of falling into the danger described by Maimonides, of pretending that God is just like us. But we may be more in danger of the opposite mistake, making Him so unlike us that He is no longer the One who told Moses He would be with him. God is not a man. But neither is He a notion or a fact or an ideal. We can never grasp His essence. But we may perhaps come to know His true and immediate presence.

> When the philosopher, Hermann Cohen, was in Marburg, he once expounded the God-idea of his *Ethics* to an old Jew of that city. The Jew listened with reverent attention, but when Cohen was through, he asked: "But where is the Creator of the World?" Cohen had no answer to this, and tears rose in his eyes.

Hermann Cohen, one of the great philosophers of the last century, understood in tears that God is not a philosophic concept. He is the "Creator of the world."

He is Someone who acts toward us. The Jew feels God's concern for him. The Jew tries to return that concern with human love. The nearness of God means very much to him. As Abraham Heschel says:

> God means: No one is ever alone; the essence of the temporal is the eternal, the moment is an image of eternity in an infinite mosaic. God means: Togetherness of all beings in holy otherness.
> God means: What is behind our soul is beyond our spirit; what is at the source of ourselves is at the goal of our ways. He is the heart of all, eager to receive and eager to give.

When Judaism thinks primarily of God's nearness and concern, it calls Him "Father." God is not our physical father. But He is something like the parent who loves us and cares for us and whom we love in return. He is with us, as He was with Moses, and we may call to Him for protection and response.

But Judaism also speaks of God as a King. He is not only like us, but also much more powerful than any man, and he not only loves us but also demands much of us, especially our obedience and respect. "King" is a word for this powerful side of God; it does not make God the same as Napoleon or George V. It only means that He is not just our Friend but also our Master. Says Claude Montefiore:

> God, then, is our Ruler and Lord. In other and equally familiar words, He is our King. What does kingship imply? It implies, on the king's side, that he cares for, and looks after, and desires the well-being of his subjects. It implies, on the subject's side, a desire to proclaim and honor the king and to obey his laws.

When we think of God as our Father we respond with love. When we think of Him as our King we approach Him in fear and trembling. When we consider God as our Friend we are filled with affection. When we remember that He is our Ruler we experience awe. The Hasidic Zusya expressed his fear of God in a most dramatic, perhaps rather strange way:

> Once Zusya prayed to God: "Lord, I love You so much, but I do not fear You enough! Lord, I love You so much, but I do not fear You enough! Let me stand in awe of You like Your angels, who are penetrated by Your awe-inspiring name!" And God heard his prayer, and His name penetrated the hidden heart of Zusya as it does those of the angels. But Zusya crawled under the bed like a little dog, and animal fear shook him until he howled: "Lord, let me love You like Zusya again!" And God heard him this time also.

Montefiore, a British gentleman, considers the fear of God much more conventional and restrained:

> The right fear of God is best expressed by the word *reverence*. For it is not like the fear that a man might have of a tiger; it is rather like the fear that a man has of his own conscience and of its disapproval.

But, of course, a person may be very afraid indeed of his own conscience. And sometimes the fear of God is also very close to physical fright. Reverence, awe, include both the animal fear which Zusya felt and the more significant emotion of which Montefiore speaks. What matters is that God is felt to be not simply a loving parent who is forced to take care of us no matter what we do or who we are. He is also free to be Himself, to be "what He will be." He will do what He

47

thinks right whether or not we wish it. And, therefore, we cannot address Him or even think of Him without fear. If we did not fear God, then the one we thought we worshipped would not be God. It would be some puny little hand-made idol which we could use any way we want. A spoiled child does not respect his parents. And God is not only a Father but also a King.

The prophets attacked the popular view of God as man's servant. They said God could and would punish an evil people, because He not only loved them but ruled them. The proper reaction to His power and justice, they said, is awe. God is Someone to fear, the only One worth fearing. Or, rather, He is to be loved in fear and trembling. Martin Buber says that, unless we realize God is not only near us but also very far away, far above our own wishes and needs, we shall end in despair when anything destroys our hope or if failure breaks into our lives:

> "Fear of God," never means to the Jews that they ought to be afraid of God, but that, trembling, they ought to be aware of His incomprehensibility. The fear of God is the creaturely knowledge of that darkness to which none of our spiritual powers can reach, and out of which God reveals himself. Therefore, "the fear of God" is rightly called "the beginning of knowledge." It is the dark gate through which man must pass if he is to enter into the love of God. He who wishes to avoid passing through this gate, he who begins to provide himself with a comprehensible God, runs the risk of having to despair of God, in view of the actualities of history and life, or of falling into inner falsehood. Only through the fear of God does man enter so deep into the love of God he cannot again be cast out of it.

God, then, dwells in "darkness." To come to Him we must pass through the gate of fear. Through fear we come near to the real God Who is no mere invention or toy. If we know that God is really high above us, then and only then will we avoid disappointment when He does not give us what we would like.

The fear of God Who is far and the love of God Who is near are not two different ways. They are man's double response to the truth that God is both Father and King. Together they make man able to know God and to do His will. Leo Baeck tells us:

> To love God and fear Him is almost *one* word in the Bible. Both in humility and in this "fear of God" there is present a sense of infinity and eternity; for the commandment, being God's commandment, is for man always unfinished. But whereas humility always has its eyes fixed on the unsearchable and the mysterious, reverence has in view what is manifest and definite—the commandment, which is always clear and always binding. In the light of duty the reverent man recognizes the endless path on which, as he passes from commandment to commandment, from act to act, he is to work out his life task.

When we pray, we call God "Our Father, our King." We mean by this that He is both merciful and just, both accepting and demanding, both around us and beyond us. Otherwise, say the rabbis, He could not be the God of men who must do His command in order to know Him.

> Said the Holy One, blessed be He, "If I create the world only with my attribute of mercy, sins will multiply beyond all bounds; if I create it only with the attribute of justice, how can the world last! Behold, I will create it with both attributes; may it endure!"

We must hold fast to both these views of God. His mercy and His justice both surround us. The prophet Malachi asked: "A son honors his father, a servant his Master. I am a Father, so where is My honor? I am a Lord, where is the fear of Me?" The religious man tries to honor God both as his Father and his Lord.

This double idea means that God's being is everywhere. Because He loves us so much He surrounds us with messages of His concern. The Rabbi of Berditchev was always conscious of God's loving presence. He sang:

> Where I wander—You!
> Where I ponder—You!
> Only You, You again, always You!
> You! YOU! You!
> When I am gladdened—You!
> When I am saddened—You!
> Only You, You again, always You!
> You! You! You!
> Sky is You! Earth is You!
> You above! You below!
> In every trend, at every end,
> Only You, You again, always You!
> You! You! You!

But it is not true that the things we see are God. As the rabbis put it, "God is the Place of the world, but the world is not His place." This means that our world rests in God, but He is also far beyond it. Like a Father, He is at home with us. But like a King, His home is also the distant palace. Judaism does not agree with the idea that God is nature. He is the Lord of nature. We see His work. We do not see all He is. Says Dr. Kohler:

Every conception which merges God into the world or identifies Him with it and thus makes Him subject to necessity, is incompatible with the Jewish idea of God, which enthrones Him above the universe as its free and sovereign Master. "Am I a God near at hand," saith the Lord, "and not a God afar off? Can any hide himself in secret places that I shall not see him," saith the Lord. "Do I not fill heaven and earth? To whom will you liken Me, that I should be equal?"

This is another meaning of the Father-King idea. God is very much with us, but equally beyond our world. The Talmudic rabbis insisted that He must be both:

A Samaritan asked Rabbi Meir: "Is it possible that He of whom it is written 'Do not I fill heaven and earth?' spoke to Moses from between the two staves of the ark"?

The rabbi said to him: "Fetch me a mirror that magnifies."

He fetched such a mirror. Then the rabbi said: "Now look at yourself."

He looked at himself and saw himself magnified.

The rabbi continued: "Now fetch me a mirror that makes smaller." The he said: "Look at yourself."

He saw himself smaller. Then the rabbi said to him: "If you, who are made of flesh and blood, can appear changed in any way you please, how much more He, who had only to speak and the world was created! Thus, if it is his will, the words hold: 'Do not I fill heaven and earth?' But if He wills otherwise, He speaks to Moses from between the two staves of the ark."

Our idea of God is paradoxical, holding fast to two apparently contradictory ideas. It also is modified by the understanding of different people. The Bible records both simple pictures of a God as a man walking in a garden, and subtle ideas of a King beyond all worlds. One Jewish teacher clings to the idea of the nearness and love of God, another insists He is far beyond mere men. One calls to a loving Father, another bows before the all-powerful King. One sees Him in loving answer to prayer, someone else in the order and majesty of the world.

We pray to "the God of Abraham, the God of Isaac, and the God of Jacob." The God of each was the same God. But, say our teachers, each man had to find God his own way, and the idea of each was unlike his father's understanding of God. This is a statement about men and how they see God differently. It is not a statement about God Whom they see.

> God said to Israel, "Because ye have seen me in many likenesses, there are not therefore many gods. But it is ever the same God: I am the Lord thy God." R. Levi said: "God appeared to them like a mirror, in which many faces can be reflected; a thousand people look at it; it looks at all of them. So when God spoke to the Israelites, each one thought that God spoke individually to him." "God," said R. Jose ben Hanina, "spoke with each man according to his power."

Men are many, but God is One. This is Judaism's central teaching about the One Who is the center of all. Jews have lived by the Unity of God, and some have died to proclaim it. You remember the words of Scripture and prayer book:

> Hear, O Israel, The Lord our God, the Lord is One. Blessed be His name whose glorious kingdom is forever and ever.
> Thou shalt love the Lord, thy God, with all thy heart, with all thy soul, and with all thy might. And these

words, which I command thee this day, shall be upon thy heart. Thou shalt teach them diligently unto thy children, and shalt speak of them when thou sittest in thy house, when thou walkest by the way, when thou liest down, and when thou risest up. Thou shalt bind them for a sign upon thy hand, and they shall be for frontlets between thine eyes. Thou shalt write them upon the doorposts of thy house and upon thy gates: That ye may remember and do all My commandments and be holy unto your God.

Why is the *Sh'ma* so important? What difference to us does it make whether God is One or not? Let Claude Montefiore answer:

This saying ("Hear, O Israel, the Lord our God, the Lord is One.") meant to our ancestors, as also to us, that besides the One God there was no other God. There is one original Divine Power, from eternity and to eternity. He is One, because there is no other God than He, but He is also One, because He is wholly unlike anything else in the world. He is therefore not only One, but also Unique. There is nobody else like Him, or that can be compared with Him. He is alone. There is no other being in His "class." He is not only one; He is the only one. And He is not only one in the sense that there is no other divine power as His partner or His rival, but He is also one in Himself. His own nature is a Unity, and there is no Unity, in its perfect Oneness, like unto His Unity. This part of the idea or belief of God's unity is much more difficult, and I do not know that I can explain what our ancestors meant by it very clearly and easily. Nor perhaps did what they meant by it exactly mean what I mean by it. For the idea is rich and not poor, and can properly mean many things, and not merely a few. But I will try and say at once some of the things which I *think* they meant by it, and some of the things which I and other Jews mean by it today.

I think they meant by it, for one thing, to imply that God was always the same. He is changeless. He does not grow or wane. He has always been, He will always be, perfect. He has no moods. He is not sometimes this and sometimes that, but He is eternally the same. He is the source of truth and the source of goodness, and being one, His truth and His goodness are changeless and permanent.

If God were not One, consider what else He could not be. He could not then be the absolute Ruler of all. He could not differ from those creatures who have a body, for only the absolute One can be incorporeal. He would be ruled by other powers and we would be ruled by many. He would be in conflict, for power conflicts with equal power. He might be the god of one nation or another; the Father of all men who are brothers must be one Father. He could not speak without contradiction to all men, different as their capacities and wishes are. He would need an idol, a physical or mental symbol, for us to know what He is. He could not be at the same time both the Father who loves us, and the King who insists on something from us.

The first part of the *Sh'ma* tells us that God is One. The second part tells us what God, the One King, demands of us. It is that we become one. We must learn to love Him with "all our heart." To do that means to build a life around the Great Center. It means to pull together all our many wishes and needs and make them all serve the One God. It means to accept His command to love Him with all we are. To love God is to become a single, integrated person. Only if we love Him, can we, too, become one.

In our Adoration prayer, we look for that day on which "God will be One and His Name will be One." Isn't He One now? Yes, but not in the way He will be when all of us come to know Him and unite to serve Him in love. Only when a man is one can he find God. Only when all men are one can God be fully One. To search out the meaning of God, for a Jew, is to accept the Sh'ma, to try to love the Father who is our King and serve the King who is our Father. The Unity of God is more than an idea; it means that God *is* our Father and our King. It means something to do, not just something to believe.

When the Rabbi of Kotzk asked where God lives, his pupils quickly answered "everywhere." But he would not accept their answer. "God lives," he said, "wherever man lets Him in."

Martin Buber, who retells this story, continues:

> This is the ultimate purpose: To let God in. But we can let Him in only where we really stand, where we live, where we live a true life. If we maintain holy intercourse with the little world entrusted to us, if we help the holy spiritual substance to accomplish itself in that section of Creation in which we are living, then we are establishing, in this our place, a dwelling for the divine Presence. . . .

It is up to us to "let God in." The only thing we can do with a whole heart is to love. And the only One who can help us love with all our soul is God. That is what He is like. That is what we discover if we let Him in.

CHAPTER FOUR

Why Do Good People Suffer?

W E BEGIN to grow up when we discover that the world is not just the way we should like it to be. And if we are religious we must ask some time or other why terrible things that can happen unjustly in our world do happen. If God is our Father and loves all men, then why does he permit good men to suffer? Jeremiah, the prophet, complained bitterly: "The good man suffers, the wicked enjoys." Why?

If the good God is truly all-powerful, then should there not be a much more direct relationship between being good and being happy? Do terrible tragedies like a small child's being run over by a drunken driver, or the murder of six million Jews, prove that there is no God at all? Some of us have very happy lives. We may be inclined to doubt that the good suffer very much. But our easy confidence is shattered when we see the tragedy of other men as our own, or when something in our own life goes terribly wrong.

This problem is one both for man and for God. It is a question which relates to our understanding of man and also of God. From the human side, the crucial principle is that of man's freedom. The ancient religions saw man as a puppet in the hands of the gods or of fate who would do with him as they pleased. Thus, there was really no problem. The gods were unpredictable; anything was possible. The good might prosper or suffer. Life was haphazard and witlessly dangerous. For a modern person who believes in fate or blind law, there is also no problem. Whatever happens, happens. Man can expect nothing from a world which is run without concern for him. He has no freedom to change things, so he should not complain about his destiny.

Judaism, on the other hand, emphasizes man's free choice, and reminds him that his choice has consequences. We are not marionettes dancing at the end of God's string. We are free and responsible persons who do what we wish but must suffer for our own mistakes. We are not incompetent children who cannot be held accountable, but mature persons who pay for their failures, and who can fail because they can also accomplish. The philosopher Maimonides wrote:

> Man has been given free will: If he wishes to turn toward the good way and to be righteous, the power is in his own hands; if he wishes to turn toward the evil way and to be wicked, the power is likewise in his own hands. Thus it is written in the Torah: "And the Lord

God said, Behold, the man is become as one of us, to know good and evil." This means that in regard to this matter, the species of man became single of its kind in this world, and that no other species is like it. Man knows good and evil out of himself, out of his intelligence and reason. He does what he wishes to do, and there is none to restrain his hand from doing either good or evil.

It is said, "Thou canst not see My face, for man shall not see Me and live"—so man has not the power to discover and to grasp the knowledge of the Creator. That is what the prophet says: "for My thoughts are not your thoughts, neither are your ways My ways." And since this is so, we have not the power to know the nature of the knowledge of the Holy One, blessed be He, his knowledge of all creatures and their doing. But we do know beyond a doubt that the doing of man is in his own hands, that the Holy One, blessed be He, does not draw him this way or that, or force him to do thus and so. And we know this not only through what has been handed down to us by religion, but through clear reasoning from the teachings of wisdom. And so it has been said in the spirit of prophecy that man is judged for what he does according to his doing, whether it be good or evil. And this is a principle on which all the words of the prophets depend.

Most of the evil that befalls individuals comes from the imperfections within themselves. The evil we inflict upon ourselves, of our own volition, and which pains us, this evil we ascribe to God. How very remote from him it is!

The Jewish answer to the problem of suffering is, in the first place, that it is an inevitable result of freedom. If man can do what he believes right, then he must suffer when he does wrong. Some Jewish writers deny that there really is any suffering at all. Since suffering flows from the nature of man and of God, maybe it only seems to hurt. Maybe pain is really a good thing for man, and his suffering only apparent. The Hasidim, in particular, thought freedom must lead only to good. Whatever came from it was redeemable; nothing was absolute tragedy.

> A hasid asked the Seer of Lublin: "To the words in the Mishnah, 'Man should thank God for evil and praise him,' the Talmudic Gemara adds, 'with joy and tranquil heart.' How can that be?" The zaddik could hear that the question sprang from a troubled heart. "You do not understand the Gemara," he said. "And I do not even understand the Mishnah. For is there really any evil in the world?"

Many Jewish writers hold that evil ends up as good because it does good for us. When we sin and suffer, that is a good thing, because it makes us better people. Claude Montefiore writes:

> Suffering brings out and develops character. It supplies a field for all sorts of virtues, for resignation, faith, courage, resource, endurance. It stimulates; it purifies. This is an old and familiar and never-to-be-forgotten truth. "The chastisements of love," of which the old Rabbis spoke, are very real. Those who have seen most of life, including its cruelties, its miseries, and its sins, have usually been, and usually still are, the firmest and strongest believers in the goodness of God. . . .

There is certainly some truth in these explanations. Freedom does lead to error, and error to suffering. And often suffering does lead to repentance and improvement. But the amount of suffering in the world cannot be explained away. It is true that wars with all their pain are the result of human failure. But what of tornados or cancer or death itself?

The rabbis were not at all sure that, apart from man's contribution to his own distress, life is really meant to be so pleasant. They argued this very point:

> Two and a half years the School of Shammai and the School of Hillel were divided on the following point: The latter maintained that it would have been better if man had never been created; while the former maintained that it is better that he was created. The count was taken and the majority decided that it would have been better if he had not been created; but since he has been created, let him investigate his (past) actions. Another version is: Let him examine his (present) actions.

Unhappiness is not always a result of moral failure. The good sometimes die young. They are often troubled by suffering which their own lives in no way deserve. The Bible notes this, particularly, in connection with the family. It quotes two contradictory proverbs: "The fathers have eaten sour grapes and the children's teeth will be set on edge." "The fathers have eaten sour grapes but their children's teeth will *not* be set on edge." Children do pay for their grandfathers' and fathers' failures. On the other hand, children should not be held responsible for their parents' mistakes.

Both of these proverbs contain truth. We all know children who are disturbed or aimless or angry because their parents failed them. Juvenile delinquency is often the result of parental negligence or incompetence. And still, none of us would willingly punish a child for something he could not possibly have avoided, for which his parents are responsible. We want each person to start life with a clean slate. But there are no clean slates in life.

Thus, say the rabbis, some do suffer for other peoples' sins. Parents do for children's and children do for parents'. All of us do for one another's. In an evil generation, it is the innocent who may be hurt the most. As the Talmud says:

> When there are righteous men in a generation, the righteous are punished for the sins of that generation. If there are no righteous, then the schoolchildren suffer for the evil of the time.

But why is it that the righteous should have to suffer for the mistakes of others in their generation? Assuming the schoolchildren are the most innocent (some of you may have your doubts), why should they be victimized? To this we have no answer except that it seems to be true. Vulgarity offends the refined alone. Violence hurts the gentle most. Sin often destroys the good man first. When we consider the history of Israel in the world, we see how often Jews have suffered for evil perpetrated by others.

Every man is free and must pay for his own errors. But, apparently, the good man pays for all mankind's mistakes. The human race is a unit. If one person drills a hole under his deck, the whole boat sinks. If one man or one group unleashes sub-atomic destruction, we will all perish.

As we have seen, the Hasidim try to deny that there is any suffering at all, in the end, that is utterly useless. What can be said in the face of this total destruction, this enormous danger to humanity, no matter how innocent some part of it may be? One attempt to moderate the suffering of the good is to remind us that this world may not be all there is. It may be that in another world, the good are finally rewarded and their suffering here on earth made worthwhile. For a time we endure and wait. But for eternity, good is rewarded and evil punished. Judaism's idea of the revival of the dead tries to explain the present injustices of this life by hope for another.

Judaism also believes that our suffering, no matter how undeserved, can lead to final good. The world is moving toward a goal. There are temporary set-backs in which suffering may be terrible. But, even on earth, this is temporary. The good will triumph in the end, and the suffering of good people is not only useful but necessary. The Messianic time will come, and, with it, both an end to human injustice and the understanding of why we had to endure so much for so long. We are doing God's will if we are good. We must not be impatient for our reward nor bitter about our pain.

But, we must still ask, and this time from the side of God, could it not be otherwise? If He is powerful and good, then why does He wait so long? Why does He let the good suffer even usefully, when He could, in the twinkling of an eye, end their pain? Montefiore says:

> As there is only one God and that God is one, it seems to follow that the universe which God rules and sustains is one also. It must be a universe which, as the phrase goes, "makes for righteousness," even as its divine Lord

is himself the source and the perfection of righteousness. Now we know that many events and occurrences on the earth are full of pain and sorrow; much evil and misery exist. But the conviction of God's unity induces us to believe, and comforts us with the faith, that the one good God *holds* the key, and *is* the key, to all the many riddles of existence. The unity of God makes us reach the faith that the same one God who is the source of goodness, is also the controller of sorrow and pain. If he sends us happiness for our good, does he not also send us sorrow? May not both happiness and sorrow, prosperity and adversity, be his messengers, and the instruments of his love?

God is, then, not only the source of our question. He is also the source of our answer. God is one and He is good, but He is not always good the way we should like him to be good. As we have seen, God is our King who will be "as He will be." He is not bound to answer all our questions, or act according to all our wishes, even the most deeply felt ones. He is God, and we are only men.

This is the meaning of the book of Job, the most important Jewish response to the question of suffering. Job sits on an ash-heap in terrible pain. He knows he has not deserved what has been laid on him. He will not accept his friends' cruel advice that he admit doing what he did not do. He refuses his wife's suggestion that he offer God a benediction (or a curse) and die. He clings to life. He clings to God no matter what has happened or may happen. "Though He slay me, yet I will trust in Him," is one translation of his agonized faith.

The end of the story seems to be a happy one. Job recovers his health and his money and has more children to love. But the real point of the story is found in the heart of his suffering. Then, when he accepts his fate while denying his guilt, when he clutches at God while God hides His face—Job is victorious. He knows that goodness will not always lead to happiness but still always will be good. He knows that the God who hurts is still God.

All of us learn that God is not our servant. We know that sometimes He seems to hide from us. Something comes between us and Him. Sometimes it is something we have made, sometimes His creation eclipses Him from us. Says Martin Buber:

> The Bible knows of God's hiding His face, of times when the contact between Heaven and earth seems to be interrupted. God seems to withdraw Himself utterly from the earth and no longer to participate in its existence. The space of history is then full of noise, but, as it were, empty of the divine breath. For one who believes in the living God, who knows about Him, and is fated to spend his life in a time of His hiddenness, it is very difficult to live.

This is the farthest point of Jewish understanding of the problem of God and evil. Even when we summarize all the possible answers we shall end with a question we cannot wholly solve. Milton Steinberg reminds us of the theories which have tried to make suffering bearable:

> 1. There are the theories which seek to account for evil in *moral* terms; among them the following:
> That an evil may be the result of some prior sin of the individual on whom it is visited; that it is often punitive even where it seems not to be, since the sin

may have escaped notice or may go unassociated with its consequence.

That it may represent the expiation of the wrong-doing not of an individual but of his community; that if a man avails himself of the advantages afforded him by his society, he must be prepared to take responsibility for its iniquities.

That it is necessary so that man may be a moral being. For how, if there were no evil, could man choose the good?

That it must be or the good would also not exist, or else, if it existed, would pass unrecognized for want of contrast.

That it is indispensable to man's character, since, were it not for its prodding, no one would ever bestir himself, let alone develop attachments to justice, compassion, and love.

That it supplies men with a touchstone on which they may test the stuff of which they are made, an adversary against whom to contend and so grow strong; a contest without which there could be no victory.

2. There are the theories which seek to account for evil in *meta-physical* terms; among them the following:

That evil has no reality in itself but is merely the absence of good.

That it appears as evil because it is seen isolated or in partial view.

That what men call evils are only instances of the laws of life which happen to strike them adversely. If they are prepared to accept the benefits of these rules, what valid complaint have they when these same rules work to their disadvantage?

3. There are the theories which seek to account for evil as something *temporary* and destined in the end to be transcended and retrieved; among them the following:

That it will be compensated and made good in life after death, and here on earth in God's Kingdom to come.

That it represents the survival into the human condition of other, lower stages of reality, mineral, vegetable, and animal, out of which man has emerged, or on which he stands; that the traces of these are being erased with time and the further unfolding of God's purpose until some day man will be perfectly and purely human.

When all is said and done, we are back with Job on the ash-heap, despairing and yet not surrendering, even when God and good seem to contradict each other.

The rabbis of the Mekilta tell us to keep looking for an answer, but not to expect all our questions to be answered. The Jew of faith thanks God for life whether life at that moment seems good or bad. God says:

Do not behave towards Me as heathens behave towards their gods. When happiness comes to them, they sing praises to their gods, but when retribution comes upon them they curse their gods. If I bring happiness upon you give thanks, and when I bring sufferings give thanks also.

Our people obeyed the Rabbinic command of God. Though persecuted and violated, they never gave up on God. The question remained which they could not answer with words. So they answered it with life. Because they knew God is, they were troubled by the meaninglessness which our world exhibits sometimes. But their response and ours must be to hold on to the problem and to find the courage to live with unsolved problems. That is what Rabbi Silver means:

Judaism frankly confronted the paradoxes which exist in theologic and philosophic thought. But while its Sages wrestled with them on the plane of inquiry, they did not for a moment slow down the pursuit of their moral objectives. Thus, for example, R. Jannai confronted with the paradox which tore at the heart of Jeremiah and Job, accepted with resignation the impenetrable enigma and admitted: "It is not in our power to explain either the well-being of the wicked or the sorrows of the righteous." However, such bafflement did not prevent this famous Rabbi from founding a school for the expounding of the Torah and for the raising of many disciples. Akiba could not solve the paradox of God's omniscience and man's free will, nor that of grace and works. This did not prevent him from dying a martyr to his faith.

The answer to suffering is living through it. We prove not only the power but also the goodness of God when we withstand pain and do not quit. Some evil is caused by man in his freedom; some leads to greater good; some is part of the very mystery of God. Not all of it is "within our reach." But in living through it we reach out to God.

CHAPTER FIVE

Why Pray?

A TEEN-AGER is running the 440 for the glory of his school. If he wins the race, Loyalty High wins the meet. If he loses, his school goes down to defeat. As he runs, he prays (silently, so as not to waste breath): "Dear God, please help me to win." He wins. Was it his speed or his prayer that won the race for him? Did God answer his prayer, or was he simply the best-trained track man in the race? What good did his praying do?

A child lies critically ill in a hospital room. Outside, his parents pour out their hearts in fervent prayer. They pray with more sincere feeling than they have ever done before. But their child dies anyway. What good was their prayer?

We must begin to answer these questions about the meaning and usefulness of prayer by trying to define what prayer is. There are many notions of prayer in the back of our minds, not all of which fit in with what we usually believe about God and the world. Some of these notions make prayer logically impossible. Here are three different descriptions of prayer which modern Jews sometimes offer. These do not agree with the Jewish tradition that we shall explore later in this chapter, but they coincide with many modern views of God. They do not, however, lead to placing much value in praying:

1. Prayer is nothing in itself. It is a ceremony whose sole virtue is that it links those who pray to other Jews of the past and living Jews in other parts of the world. It is a kind of group slogan, something like the pledge of allegiance to a flag. People who interpret prayer as a Jewish slogan, forget, however, that nearly all of their fellow-Jews of past and present meant more by their prayers than they, themselves, do now. How could prayer bind together Jews who think it is a road to God and Jews who think it is only a road to other Jews?

2. Prayer, say others, is talking to ourselves in a very efficient way. Turning our ideals and feelings outward, we can then commune with the best in us and improve whatever is imperfect. Prayer is a sort of self-hypnosis by which a person modifies his own character. It is a kind of meditation by which one reflects upon the deepest part of himself seriously and hard. But, we may ask, does this make a religious service necessary? Does it make prayer as useful as other, newer techniques for self-exploration?

3. Others think that prayer is mere superstition. They define it as a magical "Open Sesame" by which

foolish people think they can get anything they want from God if they ask Him in the correct way. Prayer, to these people, is left over from a primitive time when men believed they could coerce God by telling Him something, or cajole God by pleading with Him. Prayer, say these modernists, is incompatible with a modern religion whose view of God makes Him more than our puppet-servant. If this attitude toward prayer is correct, of course, then most of what the synagogue does is foolish or crudely superstitious.

If we reject these descriptions of prayer, it is our task to seek a better one. Here are some possible approaches which are more consistent with the traditional place prayer has in the Jewish religion:

1. Prayer is a kind of speech. It is human speech raised to its highest power, and set before God. This view agrees with psychoanalysis that there is very great power in talking, power even to transform people completely. While it does not accept the magical view that words are themselves naked force, it does accept the real and decisive nature of human speaking. If one speaks sincerely, according to this approach, if one speaks to a person and not into an empty space, the relationship of saying and hearing has the power to heal. Prayer, then, is man's speech in the presence of God, as psychoanalysis is man's speech in the presence of another human person. Human speech (of which the highest example is a confession of love) is man's greatest achievement and his most precious gift.

2. Prayer is getting ready for God to meet us. This view implies that the meeting between God and man is

the central experience of Judaism and that meeting requires preparation. Prayer, then, is a kind of school in which we learn to be ready for an experience of God. Prayer is what we do before God comes to us, so that God may come to us.

3. Prayer, say still others, is itself conversation with God. The God to Whom we can talk is, according to this idea, more like a Person than like a force. A Person can hear, though a power is both blind and deaf. We can do more, say these Jews, than prepare to talk to God or to offer our speech before Him. We can talk to Him directly and He will, somehow, answer.

These descriptions must be tested by what we know of prayer. Then we can ask, what good is prayer, anyway?

What do Jews, in fact, do when they pray? Jews do two things. They pour out their hearts, and they put something into their hearts. They express their deep feeling, and they attempt to achieve deep feeling. They talk toward God, and they hear something in return.

The first kind of prayer is praise or thanks to God for what we have. It is also a personal request which a person makes when he really needs something and thinks God cares. This prayer of expression is what the Talmudic rabbis were thinking of when they said:

> He who prays must direct his heart to heaven.
> When one prays, he must turn his eyes downward and and his heart upward
> A man should always examine himself (before offering prayer); if he can direct his heart (to God), let him pray, otherwise he should not pray.

The other kind of prayer does not express what we feel, but teaches us to feel what we first express. It is worship out of the prayer book. It is what we do most times in the synagogue. When we worship, we read prayers which we did not write. We sing tunes we did not invent. We study the Bible which we did not produce. Sometimes, perhaps slowly, the prayers become meaningful to us. The music, the Torah, the words begin to express what we would have liked to say and now can say. They began by speaking to us and now they speak for us. A Hasidic man of prayer who was called the Preacher of Mezritch said:

> You must cry to God and call him father until he becomes your Father.

The Talmudic Rabbi Simeon tells us how to make reading prayers into a personal experience. Whether the service will be boring and useless or truly personal depends on us:

> Rabbi Simeon says: Be alert in reciting the Sh'ma and the prayer. When you pray, do not make of your prayer something automatic, but a plea for compassion, a supplication before God, blessed be He.

Abraham Heschel, the leading teacher of prayer in our own time, has carefully described these two kinds of prayer:

> Prayer is an event that comes to pass between the soul of man and the word. It is from this point of view that we have to distinguish between two main types of prayer: prayer as an *act of expression,* and prayer as an *act of empathy.*
> The first type comes to pass when we feel the urge to set

forth before God a personal concern. Here the concern, and even the mood and the desire to pray, comes first; the word follows. It is the urge to pray that leads to the act of praying.

While it is true that the prayer of expression is a common and universal phenomenon, it is inaccurate to assume, as most people do, that prayer occurs primarily as an act of expression. The fact is that the more common type of prayer is an *act of empathy*. There need be no prayerful mood in us when we begin to pray. It is through our reading and feeling the words of the prayers, through the imaginative projection of our consciousness into the meaning of the words, and through empathy for the ideas with which the words are pregnant, that this type of prayer comes to pass. Here the word comes first, the feeling follows.

In the Book of Psalms some chapters begin with the words, *To David, a Psalm,* while others begin, *A Psalm to David.* The Talmud explains when David began to sing and then the inspiration came to him it was *To David a Psalm;* when first the inspiration came to him and then he sang, it was *A Psalm to David.*

In the prayer of empathy, we begin by turning to the words of the liturgy. At first, the words and their meaning seem to lie beyond the horizon of the mind. . . . Gradually, going out to meet its meaning, we rise to the greatness of prayer. On the way to the word, on its slopes and ridges, prayer matures—we purify ourselves into beings who pray.

The prayer of expression is spontaneous and natural. But the prayer of empathy is a reward for work. And both of them demand a certain kind of attitude without which prayer is impossible. What must we do to pray?

First of all, prayer requires a realistic view of oneself. It demands a great humility and a great pride. If we are not humble, we will not bow before God in prayer. If we are not also proud, we should never believe that He could care. The man of prayer thinks of himself as one who needs help. He must not be afraid of his weaknesses or his needs. On the other hand, he must respect himself enough to face God without feelings of extreme unworthiness. His humble needs bring him to prayer; his proud love enables him to stand in God's presence. It may have been meditation on man's real nature which the Talmud recalls as our fathers' preparation for prayer:

> The pious men of old used to wait an hour in silent meditation and then offer their prayer, in order to direct their heart to their Father in heaven.

Besides realism, prayer needs what is called in Hebrew *kavonoh*. That means full concentration on the meaning of what we say, true readiness for God's presence. Maimonides tells us how to concentrate in prayer:

> All such religious acts as reading the Law, praying, and the performance of other precepts, serve exclusively as the means of causing us to occupy and fill our mind with the precepts of God, and free it from worldly business; for we are thus, as it were, in communication with God, and undisturbed by any other thing. If we, however, pray with the motion of our lips, and our face toward the wall, but at the same time think of our business; if we read the Law with our tongue, while our heart is occupied with the building of our house, and we do not think of what we are reading; if we perform the commandments only with our limbs, we are like those who are engaged in digging in the ground, or hewing wood in the forest, without reflecting on the nature of these acts, or by whom they are

commanded, or what is their object. We must not imagine that (in this way) we attain the highest perfection.

Kavonoh means that we must be open and ready and free. But the third requirement of prayer, *keva*, is that balancing regularity of time and place and word which characterizes Jewish prayer. *Keva* is the fixed order of required prayer. Sabbath prayer is always on Friday night or Saturday, never Wednesday noon. Traditional Judaism requires three times a day that we turn to the traditional prayers. Even in Reform, the basic pattern of each day's worship is fixed, and the holidays are set times for special prayers. *Keva* means the continual repetition of prayers like the *Sh'ma* and the Adoration until they become our good friends. Jews may not be commanded to believe anything. But they *are* commanded to do some things. They are expected to pray over and over again in a fixed order of trying. The words are specific, the place is specific, the prayer is concrete.

> The teacher once asked his son "What do you pray with?" The son understood the meaning of the question, namely on what he based his prayer. He answered: "With the verse, 'Every stature shall prostrate itself before thee'." Then he asked his father: "And what do you pray with?" He said: "With the floor and the bench."

Keva is a problem. What shall we do if we keep reading the prayers, day after day and year after year, and they still do not mean anything important to us? What if we try over and over and we are no longer sure we are getting anywhere? Rabbi Israel Friedman told why we should keep on even when it is hard to see results:

There is a story about a small Jewish town, far off from the main roads of the land. But it had all the necessary municipal institutions: a bathhouse, a cemetery, a hospital, and law court; as well as all sorts of craftsmen—tailors, shoemakers, carpenters, and masons. One trade, however, was lacking; there was no watchmaker. In the course of years many of the clocks became so annoyingly inaccurate that their owners just decided to let them run down and ignore them altogether. There were others, however, who maintained that as long as the clocks ran, they should not be abandoned. So they wound their clocks day after day though they knew that they were not accurate. One day the news spread through the town that a watchmaker had arrived, and everyone rushed to him with their clocks. But the only ones he could repair were those that had been kept running—the abandoned clocks had grown too rusty!

We have said that prayer requires humility and pride, concentration and constancy. The highest achievement of prayer is called *d'vekus*, clinging to God, at which we have been aiming all along. For the man who knows *d'vekus*, God comes very close. The whole world is a place of prayer in which speech is miraculously renewed again and again. He is bound by his love to the whole community of Israel in which prayer has been given birth again and again. He seems to touch the garment of divinity in wonder and in joy. He is ready to speak to God in a real meeting.

But what else does prayer do for us? Does it save children? Does it win races?

Some authorities tell us that the real purpose of prayer is not to ask at all. Montefiore thinks it is simply the touching of God which we have called *d'vekus*.

Prayer is not mere petition even for spiritual benefits. It does not merely *ask* for resignation, strength, insight, humility, and the like. Prayer is also, as I have said, communion. To many persons of high spiritual purity it is more communion than petition. It is to them a sort of conversation with God; it is a sort of intense sense that they are drawing nigh to, that they are entering into the presence of, the beloved Source of Life and Goodness and Truth.

Martin Buber tells us that we cannot expect to change God by our prayer, for He is too great for that. We cannot expect Him to give us what we ask. And yet He gives us something precious—Himself. And in some mysterious way, He desires and needs our prayer.

The man who prays pours himself out in unrestrained dependence and yet knows that he has—in an incomprehensible way—an effect upon God, even though he obtains nothing from God. For when he no longer desires anything for himself, he sees the flame of his effect burning at its brightest. "Thy will be done," he says, and says no more, but truth adds for him, "through *me* whom Thou needest."

Judaism teaches that prayer does help us. It helps us to perform the commandments of the Torah. And doing the commandments, conversely, helps us to pray.

"Whoever turns his ear from Torah, his prayer is an abomination," says Rabbi Ze'era in the part of the Talmud called *Sabbath*. But the commentators on the Book of Exodus add: "Whoever performs what God wills, and directs his heart to Him, his prayer is heard."

Prayer gives us strength, if we wish strength to do what God wills. If we use it against God's purposes, prayer has no power.

Is it superstition to believe God hears prayer and answers us? Yes, if we believe that whenever we say something or do something magical, then God must jump to our command. But it is not superstitious to hope that if we call, He will hear. What would stop Him from hearing us? Why should He not hear? Magic tries to accomplish something against God. Prayer tries to tell Him something, leaving it to Him to do what He wishes. Magic accomplishes something or tries to. Prayer is itself accomplishment.

To be heard by God is to be forgiven of our errors and changed into better people. Prayer does not insure that we get what we want, but only what God wants. It cannot cure cancer or win races, but it can change lives. It has.

When we pray, our speech is carried to a high fulfillment. We who pray find wickedness embarrassing. We find that God is better than foolishness, that Torah is more precious than fun. The longer we pray, the more we find out about prayer. In the end it seems to us to be nothing less than a life shared with God. Many Jews before us have found direction and comfort and command in prayer. We may, too.

> It came to pass that once when Rabbi Susia was wandering through the countryside, he came to a crossroads and did not know which of two roads to take. Then he lifted his eyes and saw the Glory of God leading the way.

CHAPTER SIX

Is the Bible True?

How many animals did Noah bring with him into the ark? Of course, you know! It was two of each, a male and a female. The story of the Ark was one of the first you ever heard. And how many times did you draw the pictures: two elephants, two lambs, two aardvarks? Two of each, you're sure.

If you look into the book of Genesis, chapter six, verse nineteen, you will indeed find: "Of every living thing, of all flesh, two of each shall you bring into the ark to keep them alive."

But what if you happen to look into chapter seven, verse two? There you will read: "Of every clean beast shall you take seven, male and female; of the unclean animals, two, male and female."

How many animals did Noah actually bring into the ark? Two of each? Seven of the clean animals, and two of the others?

But even more important, how could the Bible contradict itself? Did God change his mind? Is one of these instructions to Noah a revision of the other? Is the second an exception for clean animals which the earlier chapter just forgot? Or is one of the commands just plain wrong?

For more than a hundred years the problems of the flood story and of many others in the Bible have raised questions like the following: How can the Bible include double-talk? How can it say different, contradictory things if God wrote it? The first chapter of Genesis and the second give different accounts of the creation of the world; how can we ever know which was "right"? Later, we read different names for several heroes like Jacob and different accounts of how they got their names. How can we know what to believe? How can we believe anything at all in the Bible?

A possible answer to the contradiction in the story of Noah, given by Christian scholars who have pondered the issue, as well as by some Jews, is this: There are two different stories of the flood in Genesis. They were written down by different men at different times. One story-teller requires the seven animals, because he wants Noah to offer a sacrifice of thanksgiving when Noah is delivered. Thus, he remembers the five extra, clean animals. But the other writer may have been very conscious that Noah was not a priest (which perhaps the author was), that Noah was not even a Jew, and therefore should not sacrifice to the God of Israel. So he felt that Noah needed only two of each animal.

Perhaps this explanation is correct, perhaps not. In

any case, we *do* find two contradictory stories of the flood. We do find other contradictions in the Holy Bible. Just as is the flood story, the Bible must be a human record. Its various parts must have been written down by different men at different times with different views on many things. The Bible is human.

This is a revolutionary admission. For centuries the Bible had been revered as an unerring spokesman of God. But if it could tell two different stories about the flood, then which should we believe? If it is full of contradictions, then why should we read it at all? And if it is a human book, then why should we give it a central place in our religion?

Even more. If the various authors lived over many succeeding years and, as people came to believe, ideas and values progress over the years, then why should the older authors or any of this old book still have any claim on our attention? Since we live in a modern, scientific time, do we not, to put it squarely, know a lot more than people who lived thousands of years ago, even if they wrote the Bible?

Most of us would agree that the Bible is a human book. That means that the man who wrote the book of Jeremiah (or at least some of what we find in that book) was a man called Jeremiah who lived at a certain time and place, and wrote in the language and ideas of his time to the people of his time. It means that the several authors of the Noah stories were men who were trying to explain something to other men. If we want to read the Bible, and then find out what use it is, we shall have to begin by reading it like any other book. Since the Bible is at least human, we must read it first as if it were any other book written by real men for real people just like us.

The wonderful truth is that when you start reading the Bible as just another book, you find out what a special and wonderful book it is. How rich in human feeling, how memorable its characters, how true to what we know about ourselves and other people! One of the reasons why so many people have read it so carefully and so long may be found in the suggestion of that Talmudic teacher with the charming name of Ben Bag Bag about Torah:

> Turn it this way, turn it that way, everything is in it; keep thine eye on it, grow old and aged over it, and from it do not stir, for thou hast no better portion than it.

This does not mean that at any single moment in our reading or in our life we will see everything in the Bible as important to us. To a young man, the love story of Jacob and Rachel may seem most appealing. To a political leader, seeking to find the best way for his people, the Ten Commandments or the Covenant Code may be central. To a poet, David's (or someone's) psalms; to a deeply religious person, Isaiah's prophecies will be precious. In any case, if we do read the wonderful collection of books in the Bible as a document of human meaning, we shall find it unique. There is nothing quite like it anywhere. But that does not mean that all of it will be important to any one of us. It only means that our belief in the Bible is a belief that even what may not appeal to *us* in the Bible may have meaning nevertheless. We do not just "take" it;

we rather give ourselves to its meaning. As Franz Rosenzweig said of the modern reader:

> Not everything in the Scriptures belongs to him—neither today nor ever. But he knows that he belongs to everything in them, and it is this readiness of his which, when it is directed toward the Scriptures, constitutes belief.

To be human can mean to be great. How human the Bible is and, therefore, how wonderful! It is not only an old book; it is also very up-to-date. It is not only a beautiful book; it also possesses great human truth. As Jacob Weinstein, a leading modern rabbi, says:

> He (the reader of the Bible) will discover the amazing relevance of the Book to the problems of our country and our times. Is he troubled by the ignorance of the masses, when mechanized processes multiply the danger of ignorance a thousandfold, and by the astounding ability of active ignorance to sell itself as common sense? Then he will appreciate a tradition that denies piety to the ignorant, that makes study a form of worship and knowledge the most benign face of God. Is he concerned with the prevalence of juvenile delinquency, the incidence of divorce, the slow erosion of family sentiment and family loyalty? Then he will profit from knowledge of a religion that has anchored its highest values to the rock of family purity and has devised its warmest ceremonies to buttress the integrity of the home.
>
> Is he pained by the coldness of human relations, by the price-tagging of human beings and human values, the slow alienation of man from man in a market-oriented society? Then he will find comfort and aid in a faith that reminds us, in every page of its Scriptures, that man does not live by bread alone, and that the noblest creature of God is the wise-hearted man. Is he

distressed by the ugly scars of racial hatred on our body politic, the denial of equal treatment and opportunity to men of dark skin? Then he will find courage to fight this injustice in the name of the God who asked: "Are not the children of Ethiopia as precious unto me as the children of Israel?"

Why is the Bible so important to mankind? Perhaps because it speaks our own language so honestly, hiding nothing, ashamed of nothing. Because it knows us so well, our agony and our triumph, our misery and our hope. The Hebrew *Tanach* is not like the Bibles of many other religions, a god-story, an epic of the birth and fall of gods and heroes. Our Bible is a man-story, the story of man as he really is.

The Bible also teaches us. It teaches us what it means to be good. Nearly all our social ideals come to us from the Bible. And they still stand out clearest in the Biblical speech, clearer than in the mixed tones of our own time. The problem of goodness is not just knowing what is good, but *being* good, making the good an intimate part of our own lives. And this the Bible helps us do, not by preaching goodness at us, but by exemplifying it, by showing what goodness can be like, in a perfectly human way.

The Bible is an old book, but it is not one we have outgrown. We still haven't reached the high morality it speaks of and speaks for. The Bible is still ahead of us, for only in the Bible are kindness and truth both human and irresistible. If we want to know what to want, what goals to cherish, the Bible is still the place for us to look.

The Bible is, then, a fully human book. As a human book, it tells of the human meeting with the holy. It discusses all kinds of themes, both the trivial and the ultimate, the day-by-day and the final mystery, the childish and the superhuman. It shows man as man.

But, sometimes, when man is most truly himself, he comes face to face with God. Sometimes he speaks about his own condition, and yet it is not only he that speaks, we feel. Sometimes when we tell what we think about ourselves, we seem to feel it is not only we who are speaking. Sometimes, Judaism tells us, the human and the divine meet in an act of disclosure called revelation. Martin Buber has tried to describe this human meeting with God's wish.

> . .. Human substance is melted by the spiritual fire which visits it, and there breaks forth from it a word, a statement, which is human in its meaning and form, human conception and human speech, and yet witnesses to Him who stimulated it and to His will. We are revealed to ourselves—and cannot express it otherwise than as something revealed.

If this notion is correct, then the human book, the Bible, speaks not only about man but, in some way, also about God. But what is it that "breaks forth" in the Biblical vision of truth? What in the Bible tells us what God thinks? Surely not the details of Noah's sacrifice, or the many scientific mistakes or the old-fashioned ideas which still lie at the bottom of many Biblical stories? What *is* divine in the Bible? No matter what greatness we shall find in the Bible, it is always mingled with the all-too-human. Claude Montefiore reminds us:

God reveals himself in different degrees to man, but the most inspired writer or speaker is still a man; his inspiration is no guarantee that he will not make mistakes. He will exaggerate; he will err; he will have his national limitations and prejudices. Even in his very conception of righteousness he will remain, in many ways, the child of his age. All this we should expect, for the divine cannot be completely contained in a human brain, a human heart, a human will. God cannot make man his secretary or his phonograph; in his perfection God remains alone. No human being can be invested with His absoluteness.

What we will find in the Bible depends on us. If we come looking for mistakes and contradictions, we shall find plenty of them. If we come to find the world lighted up and everything clearer and brighter, that can happen too. Abraham J. Heschel tells us what we must bring to the Bible if we want to take anything away:

To sense the presence of God in the Bible, one must learn *to be present* to God in the Bible. Presence is not a concept, but a situation. To understand love, it is not enough to read tales about it. One must be involved in the prophets to understand the prophets. Just as we cannot test thinking without thinking, we cannot sense holiness without being holy. Presence is not disclosed to those who are unattached and try to judge, to those who have no power to go beyond the values they cherish; to those who sense the story, not the pathos; the idea, not the realness of God.

We can only sense the presence by being responsive to it. We must learn to respond before we may hear; we must learn to fulfill before we may know. *It is the Bible that enables us to know the Bible.* Unless we are confronted with the word, unless we continue our dialogue with the prophets, unless we respond, the Bible ceases to be Scripture.

The rabbis of the Talmud believed that it takes more than the Bible to know the Bible. They saw scripture as a part of a great Jewish tradition and insisted that alone it was incomplete. Only the "Bible of the Synagogue," the written book and the oral tradition together could tell us what God wants of us:

> It happened with a heathen that he came before Shammai and asked him, 'How many Torahs have you?' He answered, 'Two—the written and the oral.' He said, 'With respect to the Written Torah, I will believe you, but not with respect to the Oral Torah. Accept me as a convert on condition that you teach me the former only.' Shammai rebuked him and drove him out with contempt. He came before Hillel with the same request and he accepted him. The first day he taught him the alphabet in the correct order, but the next day he reversed it. The heathen said to him, 'Yesterday you taught it me differently!' Hillel replied, 'Must you not depend upon me for the letters of the alphabet? So must you likewise depend upon me for the interpretation of the Torah.'

The rabbis of the Talmud and later times considered themselves the successors of the writers of the Bible, just as human but also just as indispensable to the task of discovering God's will:

> The day the Temple was destroyed, the prophetic gift was taken away from the prophets, and given to the sages.

They believed that the Bible could mean little to one who did not follow the interpretation of the later teachers and live according to the Torah. To reach the Biblical level, one must be a real Jew, humbling oneself before the law as interpreted in one's own time.

To hear God's word in the Bible, means to believe your teacher, if he is a real teacher.

Thus, the rabbis had two views of how men find out God's truth. To us these opinions may seem very different, but the rabbis insisted on both of them. On the one hand, they said the whole truth was revealed to Moses on Mount Sinai, and the whole task of man is to study the old book which God put into his hand. But, on the other hand, the law grew and moved on. The Torah is more than the written Bible. The sages are the successors of Moses and his interpreters. The teachers of the later generations may not have claimed to be as great as Moses, but still they could tell this story:

> Judah said in the name of Rab: When Moses went up to God, he found God sitting and putting little crowns on the top of the letters of the Law. He said to God, "Who is it that forces Thee to put crowns to the letters of the Law (which Thou has already written)?" He replied, "A man is to appear on the earth after many generations, Akiba ben Joseph by name, who will expound for each tip of every letter of the Law heaps and heaps of rulings."
>
> Then Moses said, "Show him to me." God replied, "Turn around." So he did, and he went and sat at the end of the eighth row (of the students listening to R. Akiba), and he did not understand anything of what was being said, and his strength failed. When Akiba came to a certain matter (which needed proof), and his disciples asked him how he knew this, Akiba replied, "This is a teaching which was delivered to Moses on Sinai." Then the mind of Moses was quieted.

Moses could not understand Akiba who lived 1500 years later, and yet Akiba claimed to be teaching

Torah in the name of Moses. The Bible (so the rabbis believed) was all there at the beginning, at Sinai, and yet it changes so completely that even Moses could not know it.

Most of us feel that the notion of the giving of the Torah at Sinai needs a careful reconsideration. We cannot picture God's revelation in so final and direct a fashion. But we are very much in agreement with the rabbis' view of the developing Torah. For us the Bible is not the last word. It is not a vision granted long-dead men that we can only read about. It is not a truth which we must only passively receive; it is a model of the kind of human life that we can still have, a life that leads to God. The Hasidic teachers understood this, too:

> A disciple of the Gaon of Vilna saw his dead father appear to him every night in a dream and ask him to give up his faith and become a Christian. Since Vilna was far away from where he lived, and Mezritch near, he decided to ask the Great Maggid for council and aid, in spite of the fact that a serious quarrel had broken out between the two schools. "Open your father's grave," said the Maggid. "In it you will find two pieces of wood lying so that they form a cross. Take them out and you will soon have peace again." And everything was just as the Maggid had said.
>
> When the man went to Vilna, years later, he told the whole matter to his teacher. The Gaon said: "This is touched on in the Palestinian Talmud. But it is astonishing that the Maggid of Mezritch understood the passage." When, after a time, the man visited Rabbi Baer, he repeated the Gaon's words to him. "Your teacher," said the Maggid, "knows it from the Palestinian Talmud, and I know it from where that book knows it."

What this strange story means is that the source of ancient wisdom is still available to men. We find God's word in the Talmud, but also in the world where the Talmudists found it. We can find God's teaching in the Bible, provided we use the Bible to understand itself, and provided that we live in the real world of which the Bible speaks. For the world and the Bible both record man's search for and finding of God.

We have said that the Bible is a human book and that it tells us how man, men like us, found God. There is also a claim that the Bible records God's search for man.

The Orthodox Jew calls this "Torah from Heaven," and believes in it in a most literal sense. He agrees with the rabbis that God spoke literally to Moses and to the prophets His own word for them to hear and to teach. Why does he feel convinced that the Bible is the literal, word-for-word quotation of God? For five reasons:

1. The whole Jewish people claimed to have witnessed Sinai, and they could not all be liars or fools.

2. The Torah admits the defects of its heroes and of the people that it celebrates. They would not have made these damaging admissions about themselves, but God would and did.

3. The style and the richness of the Bible show that no mere man could have written it.

4. The ethics of the Bible (for example, love of a stranger) is so superior to anything that the ancient Near East knew, that it cannot be explained except as a gift from on high.

5. The monotheism of the Bible is unique to this

book, and only God could have so correctly instructed the people about Himself.

Abraham Heschel also insists that the Bible is either God's word to man or a terrible lie:

> To deny the divine origin of the Bible is to brand the entire history of spiritual efforts in Judaism, Christianity, and Islam as the outgrowth of a colossal lie, the triumph of a deception which captured the finest souls for more than two thousand years. Yet, an assertion such as this would be such a shock as to have repercussions upon our very ability to make such a statement. If the finest souls are so frail, how can we claim to attain knowledge about the prophets' self-deception? What would remain for us except to despair? The Bible has either originated in a lie or in an act of God. If the Bible is a deception, then the devil is almighty and there is no hope of ever attaining truth, no reliance on the spirit; our very thinking would be useless and our efforts futile. Ultimately, then, we do not accept the Bible because of reasons, but because, if the Bible is a lie, all reasons are a fake.

The Talmud put it in one sentence:

> He who says that the Torah is not from Heaven has no portion in the World to Come.

But Samuel Cohon, writing from the Reform point of view, insisted that the Torah was man's way to God, not simply and mechanically God's way to man:

> The modern temper has effected a revaluation of the character of the Torah. Its supernatural claims cannot be maintained in the light of modern scholarship. Like the sacred writings and traditions of the other religions, so the Torah of Israel can be understood only as the manifestation of the human spirit, as the product of human needs and aspirations. Instead of being the miraculous revelation of God to man, the Torah is viewed as

the natural aspiration of man after God. Consequently neither the Written nor the Oral Torah can maintain itself as absolutely authoritative for all times and all places. Reform Judaism frankly disregards many of the provisions and viewpoints of the Torah as no longer tenable.

There are, then, two distinct views about the Bible. One says that it is God's personal, immediate word to man. If it were not, it would be the worst lie ever perpetrated. If there seem to be contradictions, these must be explained away. But the Bible must not be questioned or denied. It is what God wrote for you.

The other, liberal, view is that the Bible is part of the slow ascent of man to God, a painful human achievement of insight into God. The Bible errs and fails and can be superseded.

For a long time, these two opinions have seemed irreconcilable. Either God spoke the Bible, or man wrote it. Either it is perfect and finished, or part of an evolving understanding. Either it is literally true, or only human and imperfect. But in recent years, some have suggested a compromise between old fashioned orthodoxy and old fashioned liberalism.

They hold that the Bible is human, that human beings wrote it just the way they write all other books and, still, that it is more than all other books, even the greatest of them. It may be that only men spoke, and yet that this is the very way, the only way God speaks to men. We need not admit that the Bible is unerring to believe that it is true. We need not pretend that it is perfect to hold that it really comes to man from God. Franz Rosenzweig wrote:

We differ with Orthodoxy, because though we believe in the holiness and the uniqueness of the Torah, though we believe it is truly the revelation of God, still we draw no conclusions about its literary origins or the details of the Biblical text. If the Biblical scholars are right in all their theories (about the development of the ideas and text of the Bible), our faith would not be affected in the least. Critical scholarship calls the man who put the Bible text together from many sources R for Redactor or editor. We call him R for *Rabbenu,* our Teacher, for he is our teacher; his theology is our teaching.

What this means is: The Bible is false, and still it is true. It is false if one looks to it for geology or history or scientific fact of any kind, even though recent studies have found it capable of more historic accuracy than we used to think. It is false, if, like some Orthodox Jews, we expect it to make no mistakes. It is false, if we read it as a single voice, unchanged by time or developing human needs. It is false, if, by false, we mean self-contradictory. It is false, if we pretend that it is not human.

But the Bible is true, if we mean, by true, that it *does* speak for God. If there is a God who speaks to man, surely He could speak through this book. But when God speaks to man, He is speaking to *man.* And man can report only what he, man, can hear, not everything that God could say. God does not make man into God, so He can only meet him in a way possible for a man. The human editor and writer of our Bible (R for redactor) is also the one who collects true experience (R for *Rabbenu,* our teacher). And the true experience described in the Bible is different from experience recorded anywhere else. It is the human place where God and man have truly met.

It is important that we understand in what sense the Bible is true. But if it is somehow God's spokesman, then it also passes a judgment on us. It is not only a book that we read, and that real men wrote. It is also a book about men, about us; it is an evaluation of each of us.

That is why we must read the Bible with humility in order to read it at all. Because it is human and we are human, because it is more than human, and we can be more than we are. Because it is not only man's search for God, but also God's way to us. We turn it and turn it, but it remains forever more than we can know. What Levi Yitzhak, the Hasidic teacher, says about the Talmud, the oral Torah, is even more true of the Bible, the written Torah:

> They asked Rabbi Levi Yitzhak: "Why is the first page number missing in all the tractates of the Babylonian Talmud? Why does each begin with the second?" He replied: "However much a man may learn, he should always remember that he has not even got to the first page."

CHAPTER SEVEN

Why Aren't We Christians?

IF YOU live in a small town, you are clearly aware that most of its citizens are not Jewish. If you live in a large city, you may find that many people in your neighborhood are, but that most of the others are Christian. Large churches, both Catholic and Protestant, dominate your important streets, and the Christian calendar has become very familiar to you. You are like your Christian friends in very many ways; why, then, don't you follow their religion? What, exactly, is it that you find unacceptable to you in Christianity? And, what is your attitude to a widespread faith you cannot share?

Christianity began with a Jew, Jesus, who lived in a period between the time of the two greatest of the Talmudic sages, Hillel and Akiba. All we know about Jesus is found in the New Testament, a book composed by and for the early Christian church, and included

95

by them in Holy Scripture. Because of the nature of the book, it is impossible to separate the Jesus of history from the Christ of the church with any certainty. But most scholars, both Christian and Jewish, are confident that the real Jesus was very much a Jew of his time. Rabbi Leo Baeck, in a book on Judaism and Christianity published a few years ago, after his death, sums up the meaning of the Jewish Jesus for us Jews this way:

> We encounter a man with noble features who lived in the land of the Jews in tense and excited times and helped and labored and suffered and died; a man out of the Jewish people who walked on Jewish paths with Jewish faith and hopes. His spirit was at home in the Holy Scriptures, and his imagination and thought were anchored there; and he proclaimed and taught the word of God because God had given it to him to hear and to preach. We are confronted by a man who won disciples among his people: men who had been looking for the messiah, the son of David, who had been promised; men who then found him and clung to him and believed in him until he finally began to believe in himself and thus entered into the mission and destiny of his age and indeed into the history of mankind. These disciples he found here, among his people, and they believed in him even after his death, until there was nothing of which they felt more certain than that he had been, according to the words of the prophet, "on the third day raised from the dead." In this old tradition we behold a man who is Jewish in every feature and trait of his character, manifesting in every particular what is pure and good in Judaism. This man could have developed as he came to be only on the soil of Judaism; and only on this soil, too, could he find his disciples and followers as they were. Here alone, in this Jewish sphere, in this Jewish atmosphere of trust and longing, could this man live his life

and meet his death—a Jew among Jews. Jewish history and Jewish reflection may not pass him by nor ignore him. Since he was, no time has been without him.

When this old tradition confronts us in this manner, then the Gospel, which was originally something Jewish, becomes a book, and certainly not a minor work, within Jewish literature . . . it is a Jewish book because the pure air of which it is full and which it breathes is that of the Holy Scriptures; because a Jewish spirit, and none other, lived in it; because Jewish faith and Jewish hope, Jewish suffering and Jewish distress, Jewish knowledge and Jewish expectations, and these alone, resound through it—a Jewish book in the midst of Jewish books. Judaism may not pass it by; nor mistake it, nor wish to give up all claims there. Here, too, Judaism should comprehend and take note of what is its own.

Jesus taught many things. Some of them were certainly in the central Jewish tradition. But some were not! Claude Montefiore spent much of his life sorting out the two, and this is his conclusion:

Jesus seems to me to take up again, amid changed and in some respects more difficult conditions, some of the teaching which was put forward by the Prophets; I mean especially as to the relation of inward and outward religion to each other, and as to the service of God being shown in the service of man. His teaching in regard to retribution, to merit, to the love of one's enemy, seems to me both original and striking and to deserve the fullest and most careful consideration. His teaching respecting repentance, forgiveness, humility, and many other things, seems to me to be essentially Jewish, if not essentially original, and to present Jewish doctrine in sayings and parables of great power, beauty and impressiveness. Some of his teaching, again, is much more doubtful; it may, however, be true and valuable in the spirit though not in the letter. It requires discussion. Here I should especially allude, if I were talking to young people, to his teaching about prayer, about riches, about non-resistance. Some of his teaching, again, seems to me erroneous, involved in the limited outlook of his time. Such would be his teaching about the "strait gate," about the many who take the wrong way and are lost, about the few who take the right way and are saved, about Gehenna and its fire.

Christianity began (or continued) after Jesus in the work of Paul of Tarsus, a Jew who first attacked and then accepted the religion of the early followers of Jesus, though he had never seen Jesus alive. Under his leadership the distinctive doctrines of the church became visible, and they have never changed basically since then. Some of Paul's ideas, proclaimed in his letters to the early churches are these:

1. Jesus is the Messiah or Christ, prophesied by the Hebrew prophets and expected by Israel. He is also the Son of God, and, like any son, takes after his Father. (Christmas celebrates the Incarnation of God in human form, and Easter, the resurrection of the Divine-human Messiah who now rules with God in heaven.)

2. Man is evil and sinful. The Torah cannot save him, for it is much too difficult for man to obey the law. Only belief in the Christ, faith in an unmerited gift of God can prevent man's utter destruction.

3. The Jews were chosen by God, but they rejected Him when they refused to acknowledge that Jesus is the Messiah or Christ. Now all men who accept Christianity are the true Israel, and all others are doomed.

4. The only law for Christians is love, sacrificial giving of one's self as Jesus has done, and patient hope that God will be gracious in return.

It is enough to state these articles of faith to see that Judaism disagrees with each. For Judaism, the Messiah is still to come. For Judaism, man is *both* good and evil, and his best hope of fulfillment lies in obedience to God's commands. For Judaism, the people of Israel have *not* been rejected by God, but must continue their life and their covenant. For Judaism, love is only one of the commands of the Torah, and good deeds are its necessary expression.

Why do we believe these ideas rather than the ones expressed by Paul and the Church?

Isaac Troki in an old book written in Hebrew to "Strengthen the Faith" could see no evidence that Jesus was, indeed, the Messiah expected by Israel. He wrote:

> None of the Messianic promises of a time of perfect peace and unity among men, of love and truth, of universal knowledge and undisturbed happiness, of the end of all wrong-doing, superstitution, idolatry, falsehood, and hatred have been fulfilled by the Church.

The Christian response to this rejection is that all things *have* been changed by Jesus' coming, but that since man is evil, and the world far from Christian, the Messiah will have to return in order to prove his victory. For the Jew, however, the most important implication of the idea of Messiah is that he is still to come.

In addition, far more is at stake than whether the name of the Messiah is or is not Jesus. Christianity asserts that Jesus is also God in human form. This seems to Judaism to be a mistake both about God and about man. It diminishes the unity of God and also pretends that a man can achieve full divinity. On the one hand, it imagines God too much like man. On the other, because it claims too much for men, it leads to monastic and utopian expectations about human beings. Dr. Kohler wrote:

> Judaism sets forth its doctrine of God's unity and of life's holiness in a far superior form than does Christianity. It neither permits the deity to be degraded into the sphere of the sensual and human, nor does it base its morality upon a love bereft of the vital principle of justice.

Our dispute with Christianity is not only about what to think, but mostly about what to do. Christianity tends to deny that man's actions are very useful. Only the utter dependence on God which follows from complete despair at his own sinfulness can save man. The Jew, however, has faith that man can learn to obey God—by obeying Him, by fulfilling the *mitzvos,* the commandments. Abraham Heschel said:

> Christianity starts with one idea about man; Judaism with another. The idea that Judaism starts with is that man is created in the likeness of God. You don't have to go far to discover that it is possible to bring forth the divine within you and the divine in other men. There is always the opportunity to do a *mitzvah* (divine commandment). It is with that opportunity that I begin as a Jew.
>
> Christianity begins with the basic assumption that man is essentially depraved and sinful—that left to himself he can do nothing. He has to be saved. He is involved in evil. This is not the Jewish way of thinking. The first question of a Christian is: "What do you do for the salvation of your soul?" I have never thought of salvation. It is not a Jewish problem. My problem is what *mitzvah* can I do next. Am I going to say a *b'rakhah* (bene-

diction)? Am I going to be kinder to another person?
To study Torah? How am I going to honor the Sabbath?
Those are my problems. The central issue in Judaism is
the *mitzvah,* the sacred act. And it is the greatness of man
that he can do a *mitzvah.* How great we are that we can
fulfill the will of God!

Pauline Christianity starts with the idea that man is
never able to fulfill the will of God. All he has to do, essentially, is to wait for salvation. Here we have two different ways—the classical Jewish way, the way of the
Bible and the rabbis, and the other way. I have profound
respect for Christianity and Christian theology. Christianity is one way and Judaism is another. I as a Jew do not
know what despair is. Despair means utter futility, being
utterly lost. I will never be lost. I know where I came
from, I know where I am going. I am the son of Abraham.
Despite all my imperfections, deficiencies, faults and sins,
I remain a part of the covenant that God made with
Abraham.

Judaism does not accept the Christian notion that
man's relationship with God depends on accepting the
teaching of Paul and the Church. Judaism believes that
what man *does* will determine how near he comes to
God. Claude Montefiore wrote:

> Christianity, Jewish teachers say, declares that salvation
> is dependent upon holding that certain *doctrines* are true,
> and that certain alleged events actually happened. So far
> as this *is* the meaning of justification by faith, or so far as
> it has degenerated into meaning *this,* there can be no
> question, to my mind, that the Jewish doctrine of justi-
> fication by works is nobler, truer and more consonant
> with the goodness of God.

The teachings of early Christianity were not accepted by Jews as readily as by some Gentiles. More
and more the church became a Gentile church, with

more and more unfriendly attitudes toward the Jews. Christianity constantly appealed to the Jews to convert, and sometimes even used cruelty as its advocate. It became a world church which changed human history, but it could not ever win over the Jews. The Jew stood by his Torah and walked his own way. Writes Rabbi Abba Hillel Silver:

> It was the rejection of *all* authority to the Law and the idea of a God incarnate which placed Christianity outside the bounds of Judaism. Here was the fork of the road!
>
> Judaism rejected no treasure. Judaism rejected nothing in the teachings of Jesus, which, if accepted, would have added one cubit to its stature or in any way re-enforced its monotheism or its moral code. It was to the Gentile world that Christianity made its monumental contribution.
>
> Its moral idealism excelled anything the ancient world had to offer, but it was unlike Judaism in that it was oriented toward a Kingdom not of this world.
>
> Thus a mighty stream of influence flowed out of Judaism at the beginning of the common era and, dividing from it, watered benignly many lands and cultures. Other streams were in time to flow out of it and, again dividing, were to pursue their independent courses through history. But the river which is Judaism, replenished by the ageless springs of its own inspiration, continued to follow its own course to its appointed destiny known only to God.

According to Christianity, the Jew must become a Christian convert to be certain of salvation. According to Judaism, a Christian is "saved" by obedience to seven laws. These seven, universal laws are required of all the sons of Noah, that is, of all men. Only the Jew must do more if he is to fulfill his obligations. Here, according to Rabbinic teaching, are the only

WHY AREN'T WE CHRISTIANS?

seven universal commands which are expected of a Gentile:

1. Do not worship idols.
2. Do not practice incest or sexual immorality.
3. Do not shed blood.
4. Do not take God's name in vain.
5. Be just to men.
6. Do not steal.
7. Do not cut flesh from a living animal.

Sometimes other laws were added by individual rabbis, like not taking blood from a living animal, not offering one's child to God as a sacrifice, not practicing witchcraft. In addition, later authorities disputed the exact meaning of the Noah laws, as they did of almost everything else in Judaism. But the main significance is clear: A Christian need not become a Jew to serve God, but only must be a good man. As the rabbis often say, "A righteous Gentile will inherit the world to come."

That does not mean that Jews never made converts. The opposite is true, particularly just before the rise of Christianity. But the attitude toward Gentiles who wished to become Jewish was very mixed. In favor of conversion, the rabbis declared that Abraham, our Father, was the first of many who eagerly won souls to the Jewish faith:

> The book of Genesis tells of "the souls whom they (Abraham and Sarah) had made in Haran."
> Rabbi Elazar ben Simeon said: "If all the inhabitants of the world came together to create even one single fly, they could not put life into it. How, then, can it say, 'The souls which they had made'? But these souls are the

proselytes whom they converted. And why does it use the word 'made'? To teach you that if anyone brings near an idolater and converts him, it is as if he had created him. And why does it say *'they* made'?"

Huna said: "Abraham converted the men and Sarah converted the women. Abraham received them at his house, and gave them food and drink, and dealt lovingly with them, and brought them under the wings of the Divine Presence. This is to teach you that he who brings a man under the wings of Divine Presence is regarded as if he had created him."

The most common Jewish view is that we do not seek proselytes or converts, but neither do we make it impossible for them to become Jews.

Rabbi Samuel ben Nahmani said in the name of Rabbi Yudan ben Hanina: "Three times Scripture says, 'Return,' referring to the three times that one must repel him who seeks to become a proselyte; but if he continues to press to be received, then they receive him." Rabbi Isaac said: "Always repel with the left hand, and draw near with the right."

Still today, rabbis will accept Christians or others who wish to become Jews only after telling them of the profound and dangerous commitment that is required, and of the tragic history of the Jewish people. We are proud of our faith and of men who seek to share it, but we do not pretend that it is easy; nor do we insist it is even necessary.

Rather, our tradition has been remarkably cordial to our daughter religion. When Christians let them be, Jews usually were friendly and sympathetic neighbors. Dr. Samuel Cohon quotes a Jewish philosopher of the fifteenth century on the subject of why religions must inevitably differ, and yet why all true religions still obey the will of God:

> Why do religions differ? The Jewish philosopher, Joseph Albo, suggests the answer. He debates the question: "Can there be more than one revealed religion?" He argues that from the standpoint of God, the giver of the Law, only one religion is possible. However, from the standpoint of the recipients of the Law, there *must* be more than one, owing to the different geographic, economic, and psychic factors which enter into their lives. A religion suitable to a group of people living in a desert may not fit people who live on a fertile island. The differences between one religion and the other will, therefore, consist not in their vital essence, which is the same for all men, but rather in the secondary elements which grow out of the local and temporal variations of the characters of the groups. "Accordingly," Albo concludes, "two revealed religions may exist simultaneously among two different peoples, each leading its adherents to human perfection or salvation, though in different ways, corresponding to the character of each religion."

In the middle of the eighteenth century, Rabbi Jacob Emden praised the work of Christianity:

> Christianity has been given as part of the Jewish religion by the Apostles to the Gentile world, and its founder has even made the moral laws stricter than Moses did. There are, therefore, many Christians of high qualities and excellent morals who keep from hatred and do no harm even to their enemies. Would that the Christians would all live according to their teachings! They are not commanded, like the Israelites, to observe the laws of Moses; nor do they sin if they associate other beings with God in worshipping a Trinity. They will be rewarded by God for having taught a belief in Him among nations that never heard His name; for He looks into the heart.

Christianity brought the Hebrew Bible and Jewish ethics to the whole world. It encouraged evil men to repent and good people to cling to God. It has honestly tried to follow its master, the Jew Jesus. And even more often than Judaism, it has succeeded in arousing the artistic and poetic spirit to proclaim the beauty of holiness. Great cathedrals and great music have enriched the religious expression of the church and of the world. Saintly Christians have proved the power of the spirit in all ages. For this, Jews are grateful not only to God, but also to His servants in the Christian church.

Some Jews would go farther. They say that as Judaism is the true path to God for the Jew, so Christianity is the true path for the Gentile. They would say that Jesus does indeed "save" the Gentile and that only the Christian can bring the world to God. Franz Rosenzweig believed that:

> Christianity acknowledges the God of the Jews, not as God but as "the Father of Jesus Christ." Christianity itself cleaves to the "Lord" because it knows that the Father can be reached only through Jesus. With his church, he remains as the "Lord" for all time, until the end of the world, but then he will cease to be the Lord, and he too will be subject to the Father who will on this day, be all in all. We (Jews and Christians) are wholly agreed as to what Christ and his church mean to the world: No one can reach the Father save through him.
>
> No one can reach the Father! But the situation is quite different for one who does not have to reach the Father because he is already with him. And this is true of the people of Israel. . . .

Most Jews, however, still think that Judaism is the purest expression of what God wants of every man.

They are proud of what they can contribute to a nation of many religions, and are not afraid to state their own convictions with the utmost clarity and force. America may be predominantly Christian, but, as Waldo Frank wrote twenty years ago, it has deep need of the Jew.

> Let us never forget that a democratic nation means a symphonic nation, a nation of many voices and many themes, each keeping individuality and freedom, and yet all harmonized together. The man who thinks to benefit our country in its hour of need by wiping out the loyal differences between us ignores the meaning of democracy, and—whether he knows it or not—is tainted by the false doctrine of our foes. In union there is strength. But union implies diversity, even as strength requires diversity of forms, expressions, function. The difference of the Jew is in deep harmony with our land. For the Jew's sole special gift through the ages has been his creative loyalty to the kind of life for which we are fighting.
>
> If in our community there are Jews who openly reveal their difference as a peculiar people, let us not fear them. They belong here by an old right and a deep bond. If we run across a Jew—they are getting scarce in the United States—bearded and skullcapped, speaking an outlandish tongue or a crude guttural English, following his antiquated dietary laws and refusing to work or ride on his Saturday Sabbath, we may be sure of an ally in our cause; a veteran ally, an ally so devoted to the brotherhood of man that he has fought for it, often alone, perhaps shrunken and narrowed by the fierceness of his struggle, but ever uncorrupted, through a hundred bloody scourges like Hitler's.

Jews must wait in confidence for the day when God determines the final truth. We are grateful for our Christian neighbors, while we still resist with all our strength some of what we think they falsely teach. This is what Maimonides meant when he wrote in his great Code of Law:

> The teachings of Jesus and Mohammed serve the divine purpose of preparing the way for the true Messiah who will be sent to make the whole world perfect by worshipping God with one spirit, for they have spread the words of the Scriptures and the law of truth over the whole earth; whatever errors they cling to, they will turn toward the full truth in the time of the Messiah.

CHAPTER EIGHT

Science and Religion

WHEN we discussed the Bible we found that it sometimes contradicts itself. It is also true that the Bible sometimes contradicts other books or ideas that we trust. We should not pretend that the Bible means something that it does not mean, in order to make it agree with some other book.

In the tenth chapter of his book, Joshua is reported to have told the sun to stand still, and it did. Not only is this a rather striking miracle, but it also implies that the sun moves around the earth which, to our best modern knowledge, it does not. In the twentieth chapter of the second book of Kings, Isaiah performs a similar miracle for the King, making the sun go backward on a sun-dial. Now this cannot happen or ever have happened, if what we think about the sun and earth is true.

The opening chapter of the Bible says that God

made the world in six days. But He didn't! And it will do no good to pretend that "days" means millions of years, unless we are also willing to have Moses remain on Mt. Sinai for forty million years. This is more than a problem of what kind of book the Bible is (for the story of Creation *is* important and true if we do not try to read it as a scientific book). We are dealing with the whole problem of what *truth* is. If truth means scientific truth, that is, the combination of laboratory experiment and irresistible deduction, then how can the Bible or religion be true? If truth is found by microscope and telescope, in the theory of evolution or the theory of relativity, if truth is obviously so because it can make a new species or a new satellite, then how can God be "true"? If science is right, then is religion, too?

Some scientific people have said no, and so have some religions. Some men of science have turned their backs on religious truth (though many, perhaps most, have not). Some religious people have said, "Since it contradicts the Bible or my Church's idea of God, science must be wrong." These religions have resisted evolutionary ideas, the notion of a law of natural things which cannot change, and the new sciences of man which seek to find out what he is like. But Judaism always refuses to give up one for the other. Said Rabbi Pinhas, the Hasidic master:

> Whoever says that the words of the Torah are one thing and the words of the world another, must be regarded as a man who denies God.

Maimonides himself, the great medical scientist and rabbi, would not surrender his faith in Judaism *or* his scientific honesty. He admitted that some of our ancient leaders may well have been just plain wrong:

> We must not expect that everything our sages say respecting astronomical matters should agree with observation; for mathematics was not fully developed in those days; their statements were not based on the authority of the prophets, but on the imperfect knowledge which they themselves possessed or derived from scientists of their time.
>
> In scientific matters everyone should act according to the results of his own study and accept that which appears to him established by proof.

Many Jews have believed in miracles. The Bible records not only the sun's standing still, but a special earthquake to swallow rebellious Korah, a rock that sent forth water when Moses touched it, a donkey that could talk, and many more such interruptions of the expected order of nature. Maimonides, too, believed these had happened, for, though the Talmudic sages could be wrong, the Bible seemed infallible to him. But he carefully provided for these unexpected events in the very act of creation, thus making them only *seeming* miracles, while actually they were unusual, but still natural happenings:

> From the very beginning of Creation, God included in the nature of every created thing whatever He was going to do with it—whether it would always behave uniformly and hence in accordance with the laws of nature, or act extraordinarily, that is, be a "miracle." That is why the Sage says that on the sixth day it was ordained for the

earth to swallow Korah, and for the rock to bring forth water, for the ass to speak, and so on.

The Talmudic rabbis, who *did* believe in miracles which had occurred in Bible times and still happened in their own generation, didn't care much. There is a remarkable story told in the Talmud which indicates both their belief in the miraculous and their lack of interest in it:

> On a certain occasion Rabbi Eliezer used all possible arguments to substantiate his opinion, but the other rabbis did not accept it. He said, "If I am right, may this locust tree move from its place a hundred yards." It did so. They said, "From a tree no proof can be brought." Then he said, "May this canal prove it." The water of the canal flowed backward. They said, "Water cannot prove anything." Then he said, "May the walls of this house of study prove it." The walls bent inward as if they were about to fall. Rabbi Joshua rebuked the walls, saying, "If the learned dispute about the Law, what has that to do with you?" To honor Joshua the walls did not fall down, but to honor Eliezer they did not quite become straight again. Then Eliezer said, "If I am right, let the heavens prove it." A Heavenly voice said, "What have you against Rabbi Eliezer? The Law is always with him." Then Joshua got up and quoted the verse, "It is not in heaven." Rabbi Jeremiah said, "The Law was given to *us* from Sinai. We pay no attention to a heavenly voice." For already from Sinai the Law said "By majority are you to decide." Rabbi Nathan met Elijah, the prophet, and asked him what God did in that hour. Elijah replied, "He laughed and said, 'My children have conquered me.' "

In modern times, we are more inclined to change the whole notion of what a miracle is. Physical science itself is no longer a strict, determined order of law, but a way of looking at events where sub-atomic particles as well as galaxies act in ways that no law can ever strictly determine. Science has become used to the unexpected though it would hardly call the unexpected "miraculous." Religious people, too, have changed. Some would agree with Claude Montefiore that the absence of a miracle can be more religiously significant than any miracle ever could be:

> If I and those who think with me differ from many other Jews in not believing that physical miracles actually took place, this is not because we believe that God has *less* to do with the world, but because we believe that he has *more*. The world is so much *His* world, its laws are so much *His* laws, that there is no room or possibility for occasional suspension or change. The world is not less divine, the heavens do not proclaim God's glory less, because these miracles did not happen, but to my mind and way of thinking, the heavens proclaim His glory more.

The order of nature itself (which is perhaps more unpredictable than Montefiore thought forty years ago) is for some modern Jews the greatest miracle. The round of nature which God promised to Noah: "seeding and harvest, cold season and hot, summer and winter, day and night unceasing," is the on-going wonder. And in human life there is an even greater "miracle." As Dr. Kohler said:

> He who does not cling to the letter of the Scripture will probably regard all the miracles as poetical views of divine Providence, as child-like imagery expressing the ancient view of the eternal goodness and wisdom of God. To us also God is "a Doer of wonders," but we experience His wonder-working powers in *ourselves*. We see wonders in the acts of human freedom which rise superior to the

blind forces of nature. The true miracle consists in the divine power within man which aids him to accomplish all that is great and good.

This was understood even by those who also believed in miraculous intervention by God in the events of the natural world. Even those who thought God did divide the waters for the people fleeing from Egypt, knew that the important truth was the people's freedom and their trust in God. Even those who thought that God literally and physically made the earth in six days, knew that the central truths of the creation story are the orderliness of creation, the goodness of God and the world, the unity and dignity of man, and the centrality of the Sabbath. A miracle, then, is not a fact in the world of things, but a believing attitude of the human spirit. Miracles may not have happen*ed,* but they happen! Religious events are not facts but insights. As the Hasidic Rabbi Barukh understood, when the prophet Elijah made fire fall mysteriously from heaven to kindle his sacrifice, that was not the true miracle.

> Elijah's great work was not that he performed miracles, but that, when fire fell from Heaven, the people did not speak of miracles, but all cried: "The Lord is God."

If we wish to find out what goes on in the natural sphere, we must use scientific methods of fact-gathering, hypothesis and experiment. But when we wish to find out what the *meaning* of these facts may be, we are asking questions religiously. Scientists are authorities of fact, but each of us needs more than science to grasp the meaning of our world. Science asks "What is it?", but faith wants to know: "What does it mean to me?"

> The Rabbi of Rizhyn asked: Why are the people so set against our master Moses ben Maimon? A rabbi answered: Because in a certain passage he asserts that Aristotle knew more about the sphere of Heaven than Ezekiel. So why should we not be set against him?
> The Rabbi of Rizhyn said: It is just as our Master Moses ben Maimon says. Two people entered the palace of a king. One took a long time over each room, examined the gorgeous stuff and treasures with the eye of an expert and could not see enough. The other walked through the halls and knew nothing but this: This is the king's house, this is the king's robe! A few steps more, and I shall behold my Lord, the King!

Science may tell us *what* sub-atomic particles seem to be, *how* man can harness their power and make them work. But only when he turns to another kind of knowing called faith, does man ask *why* atoms are, *whether* they should be turned to the power of bombs or to the power of curing men's illness and filling men's needs. *Why* and *whether* are religious questions. Science may tell us how man evolved from lower forms of life, but the question, "what is man?," is a religious question (as the Psalmist knew when he prefaced it with the words "O Lord"). Perhaps, the very development of the human race as described by biology is itself a deed of God. As Montefiore says:

> What some people call development, and others call Evolution, we accept as the deliberate will of the divine Ruler. The development or Evolution *is* his deliberate will.

Because he needs truth, the religious man is a friend of science. He accepts without qualifications the right and duty of objective research. He wants to know what the world is in order that he might go beyond or within it to its Maker. He is not afraid of anything that science could ever find out, for "God's seal is truth," as the Talmud said. Reason (and science is one of reason's best organized forms) is the other side of faith. Faith is not believing what is false, but grasping the fulness of what is true. As Abraham Heschel says:

> Neither reason nor faith is all-inclusive nor self-sufficient. The insights of faith are general, vague, and stand in need of conceptualization in order to be communicated to the mind, integrated and brought to consistency. Reason is a necessary co-efficient of faith, lending form to what often becomes violent, blind and exaggerated by imagination. Faith without reason is mute; reason without faith is deaf.

The way science teaches is slow and painful, but it is God's will that we learn only that way. Montefiore writes:

> Man has acquired the consciousness of his own powers; he has gained the wish and will to discover and progress. He walks consciously with God. Each man has to some extent to decipher and unravel the universe afresh. God has placed the incentive within man, so that he must and can, with God's help, work out his own salvation. We know the best human teachers make their pupils to some extent teach themselves. May not the divine Teacher have reason to teach us in the same way? The greater the knowledge and the faith which we have to acquire, the longer must be the pathway, the more painful the experiences, which are needed to acquire them.

We moderns are Jews in a new way, a way that was not possible before the birth of modern science. We learn in a new way, we can no longer take for granted the old wisdom, but must begin in the modern world with the truths of our own time. Physics, biology, psycho-analysis are not only names of scientific disciplines. They are also the names for roads that can lead to God. Science asks questions perpetually, and perpetually revises the answers it gives. But these are questions that lead to even deeper ones which science can never answer. The whole purpose of seeking truth is one that science itself cannot justify, but which is a principle of faith. Trust in the orderliness of the world is an act of dedication common to both science and religion. As Einstein, the greatest physical scientist of our century, affirmed, "God is very subtle, but He does not deceive." That truth is possible, that mind is significant, that science is not just a game, depends on a faith that science itself cannot provide.

The modern Jew accepts the world of modern science, but he does not stop with it. He plunges deeper and deeper into the heart of things until he arrives at the wondrous center which we call Torah, the instruction from God. This is what Franz Rosenzweig meant when he said:

> A new "learning" is about to be born—rather, it has been born.
> It is a learning in reverse order. A learning that no longer starts from the Torah and leads into life, but the other way round: from life, from a world that knows nothing of the Law, or pretends to know nothing, back to the Torah. That is the sign of our time.

It is the sign of our time because it is the mark of the men of the time. . . . All of us to whom Judaism, to whom being a Jew, has again become the center of our lives—and I know that in saying this here I am not speaking for myself alone—we all know that in being Jews we must not give up anything, not renounce anything, but lead everything back to Judaism. From the edge back to the center; from the outside, in.

Science is the "outside" of modern life. But deep, at the inner heart of things, God still is found. The modern Jew, in studying science, moves into the depths of religious faith.

CHAPTER NINE

Ceremonies and Commandments

A GIRL in a confirmation class I taught once defined conscience as "what feels so bad when everything else feels so good." She was hinting at the fact that conscience (just like the commands of religion), is often the contrary of our own desires. The person who observes the Ten Commandments does not do so because it is always easy or pleasant. Rather, the Bible tells us, a great many impulses make us want to worship idols, to covet other men's things, even to kill. These wishes of ours are opposed by the belief that God wants us to obey the Commandments.

The same thing is true about the so-called ritual ordinances of Judaism. The Orthodox Jew is commanded not to eat pork even though he wants to. The Talmud says that a good Jew really *does* want to eat forbidden foods, but abstains anyway. A good Jew might sometimes prefer to desecrate the Sabbath or to cheat just a little in business. But he feels that God wants him to keep the Torah. The Talmud says that it is *better* to do a good deed under the impulse of God's law than to do it just because we feel like doing it:

> Rabbi Hanina teaches: Greater is he who is commanded and obeys, than he who does good without being commanded.

And still, few of us keep the Commandments exactly as they are written. We do not do everything that the Bible says to do, much less what the Talmud or the code books direct. We say that we do not keep them, because we think they are no longer what God wants of us. He may have wished the early Jews to let their beards grow, or to kill witches, but these Biblical laws do not seem to us any longer worthwhile or instructive. Sometimes we say that the meaning of being liberal Jews is that we can choose for ourselves which laws we will accept and which we will not. It is only the Orthodox Jew who knows what he should do (even if he doesn't always do it) just by looking in the right place in the right book.

But if *we* choose what laws we think are binding upon us, then what makes them laws at all? If *we* decide what God wants us to do, then how can we be sure it is He who is giving the orders, and not we ourselves making up the rules as we go along?

Who makes the laws in Judaism: God or man? Who decides what we should do? God or we ourselves?

This is a problem as old as the Bible. Sometimes, in

our tradition, the power of man's decision is emphasized, sometimes God's over-riding, imperial order; sometimes we hear of man's creation of the Law, sometimes of God's command.

In the book of Nehemiah, this is the description of how the Jews came to accept the Torah:

> All the rest of the people, the Priests and Levites, the gatekeepers and singers and temple-servants, all those who had separated themselves from the people of the lands toward the Torah of God, their wives and their mature children, everyone with knowledge and insight, supported their brothers and their nobles and came into an oath under penalty of a curse, to walk in the Torah of God which was given by Moses, the servant of God, to observe carefully all the commands of Adonoi, our Lord. "We take upon ourselves the commandments." (they said).

We read here in Nehemiah how our fathers "took upon themselves the commandments," deciding for themselves what God wanted, and together agreeing as to what they would do about it. But in the Book of Exodus we read the more familiar story of how the Commandments came down from Heaven to earth:

> All the people perceived the thunders and the lightnings and the sound of the Shofor and the smoking mountain. All the people saw and trembled and stood off at a distance. And they said to Moses: Speak with us and we shall hear, but let God not speak with us or we perish! And Moses said to the people: Do not be afraid, for God has come to test you that fear of Him might be on your faces, that you would not sin. And the people stood at a distance while Moses drew near to the thick darkness where God was. And *Adonoi* said to Moses: Thus shall

you speak to the children of Israel. You have seen that I have spoken to you from heaven. . . .

The same differences of emphasis are found in the Rabbinic teachings. On the one hand, it is told that Israel chose the Torah, and that in fact, they were the only people who did:

> Why did the Holy One, blessed be He, choose Israel? Because all the peoples repudiated the Torah and refused to receive it; but Israel agreed and chose the Holy One, blessed be He, and His Torah. When the all-present revealed Himself to give the Torah to Israel, not to them alone did He manifest Himself but to all nations. He first went to the sons of Esau, and said to them, "will you accept the Torah?" They asked what was written in it. God told them, "Thou shalt not murder"; and they replied, "Sovereign of the Universe! The very nature of our ancestor was bloodshed; as it is said, 'the hands are the hands of Esau' and for that reason his father promised him, 'By thy sword shalt thou live.' " He then went to the sons of Ammon and Moab and said to them, "Will you accept the Torah?" They asked what was written in it. He replied, "Thou shalt not commit adultery." They said to Him, "Sovereign of the Universe! The very existence of this people springs from an act of unchastity." He went and found the children of Ishmael and said to them, "Will you accept the Torah?" They asked what was written in it. He replied, "Thou shalt not steal." They said to Him, "Sovereign of the Universe! The very life of our ancestor depended upon robbery." There was not a single nation to whom He did not go and offer the Torah; for thus it is said, "All kings of the earth shall give Thee thanks, O Lord, for they have heard the words of Thy mouth."

But another Talmudic story tells that even the Jewish people did not want to accept the commands that God forced them to heed His word.

> The Holy One, blessed be He, turned Mount Sinai over them like a huge vessel and declared, "If you accept the Torah, well and good; if not, here shall be your grave."

Why did God want us to accept His command? Sometimes the rabbis come very close to saying that God does not really care about the *ritual* law for Himself, but only gave it for man's own improvement:

> What does God care whether a man kills an animal in the proper way and eats it, or whether he strangles the animal and eats it? Will the one benefit Him, or the other injure Him? Or what does God care whether a man eats unclean animals or clean animals? The Commandments were given to purify God's creatures.
>
> Rab said: "The commandments were given to Israel only in order that men should be purified through them. For what can it matter to God whether a beast is slain at the throat or at the neck?"

The concern of the Rabbinic law for what man needs gives Torah a very human flavor. We are each commanded, in the Rabbinic phrase:

> Make yourself holy by doing what is proper for you.

On the other hand, if we try to find reasons for observing the law, if we try to reduce the Torah to merely human education, then we find the rabbis insisting that it also serves *God's* purpose which is closed to human understanding. If we ask why we should observe the traditional and mysterious laws of purity and impurity, for instance, we can receive no answer, for this is God's business and not ours:

> The dead body does not really defile; the water does not really purify; but God has said, "I have ordained an

ordinance. I have decreed a decree; it is not permitted to you to transgress it."

These two approaches to the question of Jewish law, one emphasizing human choice, the other emphasizing Divine direction, both continue throughout Jewish history. The Hasidic teachers, for example, who sought to make Judaism an intense personal experience, did not think that even God would make a single law for all men, nor that all men were in need of the same instruction from God:

> Rabbi Baer of Radoshitz once said to his teacher, the rabbi of Lublin: "Show me one general way to the service of God." The zaddik replied: "It is impossible to tell men what way they should take. For one, the way to serve God is through the teachings, another through prayer, another through fasting, and still another through eating. Everyone should carefully observe what way his heart draws him to, and then choose this way with all his strength."

Those who see the Jewish system of practice as a way of training men primarily, find many reasons even today for observing the rituals and customs of their people without assuming that this observance has any other-worldly or divine significance. Consider the reasons for observance summarized by Rabbi Milton Steinberg:

> 1. *Judaism as a Way of Life.* Judaism, being more than a church, is broader in its interests than theology and ethics. It is, in fact, no less than a full way of life, wherefore it seeks to mold not only the beliefs, morals, and worship of the Jew, but his every act, his eating, drinking, work, and play. Ritual is the instrument designed to this end, carrying the Jewish religion into every nook and

cranny of his being until nothing he does is untouched by Judaism.

2. *The Sanctification of Life.* A key objective of Judaism, as we have already observed, is the sanctification of life. Every moment, the Tradition contends, ought to be suffused with the awareness of God and with moral fervor. To this end each turn of man's existence should be accompanied by acts evocative of religious and ethical idealism. Under this conception, Jewish ritual is indeed intended as a spiritualizing device, a kind of persistent and all-pervading whispering of the verse in Numbers: "And ye shall look upon this and remember all the commandments of the Lord."

3. *Ritual as Discipline.* "The prime purpose of the commandments," said an ancient rabbi, "is to purify human nature."

Religion, like everything else, has to be tended if it is to matter. Regular seasons must be set aside for it, as for any other serious interest, and during these times prescribed exercises must be performed.

The effectively pious man then is very likely to be none other than the one who toils over his religion according to a program of specified acts at stated hours.

4. *Ritual as Pedagogy.* Observance is a form of instruction and one of extraordinary effectiveness. It educates not on random occasions but constantly. It employs the sound technique of teaching by action rather than with words. It deals not in abstractions but in their tangible expression. It operates everywhere, as much in the home as in the synagogue, and in the market place, too. It is understood by all: the child and adult, the naive and the sophisticated. All in all, it may well be religion's best single instrument of indoctrination.

5. *Ritual as Participation in the Historic.* To specify: A Jew will feel most thoroughly identified with the career of his people and faith when he observes the Sabbath, celebrates the Passover feast, or stands in the presence of the Torah scroll; that is, on the occasions when his hand as well as his head and heart is busy with the gestures

which in their generations his forefathers executed and which in time to come will be performed by his descendants also.

6. *Ritual as Fellowship*. By the same token, a man's solidarity with his fellows is firmest when he and they act together and alike. Never is a Jew surer of himself as a Jew than in the hours when all Jews everywhere engage in identical acts—on Passover Eve, for example, or on the Day of Atonement. What is more, he will tend to be stronger in his convictions for the knowledge that he does not stand alone in either faith or its expression, but that those like-minded with him make up a numerous and distinguished company.

7. *Ritual as an Aesthetic*. What poetry and music are to language, that Ritual is to conduct. Onto the hard-headedness and practicality of existence it throws a splash of color and passion. Candles are lit, spice boxes are sniffed, rams's horns blown, liturgies intoned; a past revived, and unborn future anticipated. This, not the prose of living, affords a man many of his softest, dearest memories and evokes from him emotions not otherwise to be duplicated. In a word, ritual is one of the arts whose cultivation lends beauty to living.

8. *Ritual as Survival Mechanism*. A minority communion everywhere, Judaism is exposed to the corrosives of other faiths and cultures. Against ever-threatened dissolution, ritual serves as a shell, enfolding and protecting tender inner parts and the spirit that informs them.

But, despite these persuasive arguments for ritual observance, there is no doubt that, since the fall of the ghetto, Jews have tended to give up many of the old practices sanctioned by Judaism.

Some Jews are delighted with this development, which, they believe, brings us closer to the non-Jewish community, and reduces our appearance of being different. But some, who agree in putting the value of

Jewish ceremony in human terms, regret that we have given up so many customs which might still offer something to the Jewish person of today. Foremost among the latter group is the Reconstructionist Movement founded by Dr. Mordecai Kaplan. The Reconstructionists have sought to rebuild the structures of Jewish life without calling upon any sanction outside the world of men. They have insisted that the two decisive reasons for keeping some of the old commandments, reinterpreting them for today, and even adding new ceremonials, are that they fill personal needs, and that they keep alive the Jewish impulse to survive. This, and no more, constitutes for them a relationship to God. Here is part of the Reconstructionist pamphlet titled "Toward a Guide for Jewish Ritual Usage":

> The Reconstructionist position is that, in the matter of ritual observance, as in so many other phases of life, it is necessary to strike a balance between the interests of the group and the interests of the individual. This is implied in the fundamental principle of Reconstructionism which not only identifies the individual with his group but makes the group responsible for the salvation of the individual, for helping him to experience life as supremely worthwhile or holy and thus to commune with God. A satisfactory rationale for Jewish usage is one that would recognize in it both a method of group survival and a means to the personal self-fulfillment or salvation of the individual Jew. Through it, the individual Jew will know the exhilaration of fully identifying himself with his people and, thereby, saving his own life from dullness, drabness and triviality. Jewish tradition brings to the daily living of the Jew, to his holiday celebrations, to the celebrations of turning points in his life, a wealth of beautiful and meaningful symbols embodying the

sancta of his people, expressive of its ideals and native to its culture. These should be retained and developed, for no creed, no value, no self-identification of the individual with his people is effective except as it is translated into action of a systematic and habitual nature.

If we accept this rationale of Jewish usage and recognize its dual function of contributing both to Jewish group-survival and to the personal self-fulfillment of the individual, we must accept as a corollary the sanctioning by the group of variations in ritual usage. The circumstances of life are so different for different Jews, their economic needs and opportunities, their cultural background, their acquired skills and inherited capacities are so varied that it is unreasonable to expect all of them to find self-fulfillment in the same rituals. That was possible only where the Jewish community lived a self-contained life and could make possible for all its members, without undue sacrifice on their part, the observance of all usages which were the norm in Jewish life. It is not possible where, as in democratic countries, the Jew has to live in two civilizations and find his place in the economic and cultural life of the civic community as well as of the Jewish.

From this point of view no stigma attaches to those who permit themselves a wide latitude in their departure from traditional norms. Adherence to tradition is henceforth to be evaluated not solely in terms of group needs but also in terms of individual satisfactions. It certainly cannot be considered in terms of a super-naturally revealed code.

For those who have been trained to think of ceremonial observances as divine commandments or as part of a self-sufficient, mystic "law" which is the essence of historic Judaism, the elasticity of this new approach will, at first, seem unsatisfactory. There is, however, literally no alternative. Modern thought acknowledges the propriety of the concept of law only in nature and in human relationships. In the sphere of ritual, of the relationship between man and God, there can be no law. A modern

state is separated from any established church and refuses to legislate on matters of religious practice.

But to deny that ritual usage can appropriately be
treated as law does not mean that it can be left solely
to the individual to deal with. For the benefit which the
individual hopes to derive from ritual usages is dependent
on their power to effect his self-identification with the
Jewish group. Consequently, it is important for those who
feel the need of such self-identification through ritual
to evaluate the heritage of traditional Jewish usages and
to adopt those that are capable of functioning benefi-
cently in their lives. Moreover, since the obsolescence of
much traditional usage is inevitable, they would also do
well to consider the possibility of introducing new usages
that can similarly contribute to self-identification with the
Jewish people and to personal self-fulfillment as Jews.

The Reconstructionist approach has made itself felt
in both the Conservative and Reform branches of
Judaism. Observers have noted, especially among Reform Jews, an unexpected return to Jewish ritual and
ceremony. Recently, without claiming that Jewish
practice is of any direct benefit to God, some Reform
Jewish writers have urged that Jewish observance is of
the highest importance to the Reform Jew himself.
Here is a part of Rabbi Morton Berman's report to the
1950 General Assembly of the Union of American
Hebrew Congregations, the national body of Reform
Judaism:

> Our study reveals widespread and increasing accept-
> ance by congregations and their members of ritual prac-
> tice and ceremonial observance. It demonstrates that Re-
> form Judaism is determinedly engaged in helping to
> meet a fundamental need of every human being for sym-
> bolism and ceremonialism in his religious life. It provides
> striking evidence that our movement has undertaken to

correct a most costly error made by the early anti-ritual-istic Reformers who were earnestly intent upon emphasiz-ing ethical and religious principles and righteous conduct but looked upon "the ceremonial system to be a trivializ-ing of the noble teaching of Judaism . . . and the deep learning involved in the study of it . . . as a wastage of intellectual capacity, and an alienation from the broader culture in the modern world." This apt characterization of the attitude of the primarily anti-ritualistic Reformers was made by Dr. Solomon B. Freehof in a brilliant ad-dress before the 1950 meeting of the Central Conference of American Rabbis.

The error on the part of the early Reform Movement led to the elimination of many practices. Opposed as the Movement was to ritualism, it was obvious that it was not minded to reconstruct any of the practices or to pro-vide substitutes for them on the basis of the needs of the people in consonance with the changed conditions under which Jews lived. The early builders of our Movement failed to recognize that man cannot live by reason alone, that he needs to sate his emotional hunger for the poetry and beauty, for the mysticism and drama which are to be found in meaningful symbolism and ceremonialism. Those who dispensed with ritualism did not perceive that religious practices and observances are means for the fortification of the Jew's faith and for the stimulation of his will to serve God and do His commandments. They were indifferent to the importance of the act as well as of the word to a full religious life. They were unaware of the role that ritualism plays in helping a Jew find identi-fication with his group and self-fulfillment in his personal life.

Our study demonstrates that a new attitude pervades our Movement with respect to the significance of ritual and ceremonial observance. It is now generally recognized that these disciplines have the power to restore in the Jew a sense of kinship with God, because they are re-minders of the providential role that He filled in His people's life throughout the ages; that they help the

Jew to relive his history which has always been a vital source of support for his faith and a bulwark for his self-respect; that they instill in the Jew faith in despair, as they did for his fathers, and strengthen him to triumph psychologically and spiritually over every defeat.

It has become clearer to us also that ritual practices and ceremonial observances give the Jew a sense of rootage in his people's past, but they also fill him with a fortifying sense of union with all other Jews of our time who engage in these practices. George Foot Moore, in his great work on Judaism, pointed out that the worship in which Jews everywhere participated and the observances universally shared by them were bonds which always united them. The feeling of inseparable relationship with our past and our present, which can be nurtured by the use of our symbols, our ritual practices and ceremonial observances, is a necessary condition for the survival of the Jewish people and its inheritance.

As Dr. Freehof pointed out in the address previously cited, it is not easy to explain adequately why Reform Judaism has moved toward ritual and ceremony, but what he said there appears to be a most satisfactory explanation: "Perhaps there has been a general shift in the world atmosphere from classicism to romanticism, and so in the English Episcopal Church there has been a shift from Protestantism to a sort of ritual Catholicism, the drama without the doctrine. But with us there has been another element which tended to bring anti-ritualistic Reform back into the ritual mood. The Zionist movement, the new interest in Chassidism, and a number of similar factors have added a folk-feeling to our theology. We began to be interested not as hitherto, only in Judaism, but also in Jewishness."

But not all modern authorities agree that Jewish practice has a merely human significance. Abraham Heschel believes that to turn a law which comes from God into a mere custom chosen by men because it serves some need of theirs, is to misunderstand the meaning of Jewish law. For him it is only *mitzvoh,* the commandment from God that is important, and not *minhag,* the custom or ceremony which some Jews may invent to keep themselves feeling close to their fellow-Jews, or may revive to guarantee the survival of the Jewish people. Dr. Heschel writes:

> There are spiritual reasons which compel me to feel alarmed when hearing the terms *customs and ceremonies.* What is the worth of celebrating the Seder on Passover Eve if it is nothing but a ceremony? An annual re-enactment of quaint antiquities? Ceremonies end in boredom, and boredom is the great enemy of the spirit.
>
> A religious act is something in which the soul must be able to participate; out of which inner devotion, *Kavanah,* must evolve.
>
> Let us be frank. Too often a ceremony is the homage which disbelief pays to faith. Do we want such homage?
>
> Judaism does not stand on ceremonies. . . . Jewish piety is an answer to God, expressed in the language of *mitzvoth* (commandments) rather than in the language of *ceremonies and symbols.* The *mitzvah* rather than the ceremony is our fundamental category. What is the difference between the two categories?
>
> Ceremonies whether in the form of things or in the form of action are required by custom and convention; *mitzvoth* are required by the Torah. Ceremonies are relevant to man; *mitzvoth* are relevant to God. Ceremonies are folkways; *mitzvoth* are ways to God. Ceremonies are expressions of the human mind; what they express and their power to express depend on a mental act of man; their significance is gone when man ceases to be responsive to them. *Mitzvoth,* on the other hand, are *expressions or interpretations* of the will of God. While they are meaningful to man, the source of their meaning is not in the

understanding of man but in the love of God. Ceremonies are created for the purpose of *signifying: mitzvoth* were given for the purpose of *sanctifying.* This is their function: to refine, to ennoble, to sanctify man. They confer holiness upon us, whether or not we know exactly what they signify.

A *mitzvah* is more than *man's reference to God:* it is also *God's reference to man.* In carrying out a *mitzvah* we acknowledge the fact of God being concerned with our fullfillment of His will.

Leo Baeck, the great liberal Rabbi, also emphasized the idea that the commandment comes *to* the Jewish person, not *from* him, that it comes to him again and again, directing him to do more than he wishes, not just satisfying a need, but creating one that never can be wholly filled:

> If man is to be holy as God is holy, or, as another Biblical expression has it, if he is "to walk in all His ways and to love Him," if his life is to be thus measured by the supreme, divine standard, his task is never finished. The commandment comes to him as something that is ever new; commandment follows commandment; man is never done with it. The ideal continually rises up before him, demanding to be realized, and yet it ever recedes before him into infinity.

Rabbi Baeck here puts the emphasis on man's relationship not with himself nor with his people, but with God. The purpose of Jewish obedience is to follow God's way, to learn to be holy. The demands of the Jewish life come from beyond our world, though they must be fulfilled in our world. God sets the standard, and man must try to follow it, even though he knows he cannot fully succeed. This is what the author of

Judaism's most famous code, Joseph Karo wrote centuries ago:

> It is the duty of man to turn his eyes and his heart to his path, and to weigh all his doing in the balance of reason. If he sees something that will lead to serving the Creator, blessed be He, let him do it; if not, let him not do it. Whoever keeps to this, will be constant in the service of his Creator.

How shall we choose between these opposite emphases? Is the ceremonial and ethical system of Judaism a command that comes to man from God, or is it man's personal achievement? Is it a divine direction or the Jew's attempt to find his way to his people and to the meaning of their survival? Is it what God wants of us or just what we think is worth doing?

This question is much like the one we discussed in connection with the question of whether or not the Bible is true. We asked whether the Bible is God's word to man or man's picture of God. And the answer we arrived at was: both! The Bible is written by men, real men, men like us, but it is written out of their burning personal relationship with the living God. So, too, the laws of Judaism (which are found in the Bible and in later Jewish sources) were devised by men, but by men who were creating out of a sense that they were commanded. Jewish law is not mere custom, but also direction, Torah, a way not wholly invented by man. The honest Jew will not breezily pick and choose among the many attractive products of the Jewish heritage as he would packages in a super-market, though he still cannot accept all of the old law. He studies and tries and wonders, and somehow discovers slowly what God wants of him. This honest search was beautifully described by Franz Rosenzweig in a letter he wrote on his deathbed on March 27, 1922:

> Do you really think it's so hard to live up to the law? But, just look at the people who do! It's a mild sort of law, really, and I could manage it tomorrow if I wanted to, by simply keeping all the commandments, I could bypass the central problem of my life.
>
> Don't you see? If I were to accept the traditional law as made to order for emancipated, Western Jews by the leader of the New Orthodoxy, Samson R. Hirsch, what would my so doing mean to you? May I answer directly: you would look at my observing "everything," and be quite satisfied to claim "nothing" for yourself. Many do that today. I am opposed to the notion of "all or nothing." Neither "everything" nor "nothing" belongs to us, but rather "something." Something has been given to us: we must adapt to "something." I do not say that my "something" should be a model for someone else, but it is a model that I have the courage (against the alternative of "everything" or "nothing") to live with. I do not know the details, yet; I'm just beginning. I do not know what it will grow into, and I do not want to know. I hope, and I know, that others are trying also, and that a model will come out of our combined efforts.
>
> I, we, all of us who do not say "everything or nothing," will try to do today what early Jewish liberalism failed to achieve a hundred years ago. It failed, because it first wanted to set up principles and then to live up to them. The principles and those who fought for them remained officers without soldiers, fathers without children. We will begin with doing, maybe later we or others will find the principles.
>
> What right do I have to begin without principles, without a system? Judaism is not law; it only creates Law. But it is not itself law. It is: *to be a Jew!* That is what I

wrote in my book, *The Star of Redemption*, and I know it is correct. But now I see that life begins only after the book is finished, living up to it follows the theory. The old saying "These are the laws by which a man shall live." Live, that is, and not die—this saying shall be above any detail of the Law, a rule if there is to be one at all. "Something" will be possible for one person which is impossible for someone else. My way is mine only, but I know I am a comrade of everyone who is going his own way. If only he *goes!* If only he does not wait for "everything" to come, or wait with a lazy "nothing" for a call to sound which never will come.

To know that I am allied to everyone who is seeking is not mere knowledge, but my goal. In fact, it is my only real goal. My *way* has to be my own, a Law I can live by, live in a more intense fashion. But the goal means that my knowledge is accessible to everyone. I cannot shirk my duty to learn all about living according to the Jewish way wherever I see it, in the past or in the present. I have to love the way as a brother. Not that I must, God forbid, love "every Jew," but only the thousands of ways within Judaism. I must connect their way with my way. I have to learn to love their way, for they are "like myself."

This kind of love will have consequences for my life and for my Jewish way. There is no danger that it will lead to isolation, for all the ways are in the same landscape.

Once there was a road for all Jews, a universal road with clover-leafs and bridges and towns, but the single road is gone; it has not existed for a hundred and fifty years. Now it is only one among many roads, no longer *the* highway. So we must trust to the unity of the landscape. Someday a great road may run through it again, but even that will surely not be the only one. And all our little, personal roads are real preparation for the future way.

"Waiting" for the answers won't do. You must go out to meet what you actually need. If you really want it, look around, live with other Jews of past and present, look for openings—if you are not just plain lazy—then a day will come when you can do things only in a certain way, and this way will be your own, a perfectly natural "something" for you.

Torah-law, for the Jew, comes out of a relationship with God. We all have different relationships, and so what we should do may be somewhat different. But all our lives are part of the Jewish "landscape" and our total obedience to the one God adds up to Torah.

Some liberal Jews think the time is ripe now for a code of practice stated by scholars and freely chosen by any Jew who wants to live by it. They believe that, even today, Torah will come to our people if we are very attentive to God's call. And what will be the test of whether a *mitzvoh* is really spoken by God to us or not? Rabbi Frederick Doppelt and Rabbi David Polish in their "Guide for Reform Jews" have suggested a criterion:

> . . . We need only inquire whether the *Mitzvot* we are to keep constitute spiritual moments in Jewish history when the Jewish people came upon God . . .
>
> By *Torah mi-Sinai* (law from God on Mount Sinai) we mean that Torah comprises historically spiritual life-processes wherever and whenever the people Israel stands at Sinai and hears the voice of God.

A real commandment can only come at Sinai, which is, however, anywhere God and man meet; any moment in the life of the Jewish people can become a Sinai. Any great experience that our people undergoes (the martyrdom of millions, the birth of the State of Israel, the confirmation of hundreds of our young people) can bring new orders to us from God. And any Jew who tries to live in a way both personally and Jewishly honest, will find a *Torah* coming out to him. We cannot predict just what that *Torah* will be, nor are we simply to wait lazily for it to come to us. But in going out to meet the commandment, we may also find the One who commands. Commandments are the effect of both God's work and man's. In working out what we must do, we shall discover who we are, and, perhaps, who God is, too.

CHAPTER TEN

An End: a Beginning

WE ARE nearly at the end of our year's journey. You have thought and spoken about some of the most difficult and important questions in the world. You have read some of what the Bible and the Talmud, the Hasidic teachers and philosophers, modern rabbis and the disciples of the wise have had to say about these perplexing problems. You have tried to come to your own notions of God and of His world.

Soon you will be confirmed. You will stand before your parents and your congregation with your Rabbi and your teachers at your side, and join forever the fellowship of Judaism. You, yourself, will now have to begin to be a teacher as well as a disciple.

May I guess how you feel as your journey nears an end? Perhaps as the old commentator on the Psalms did:

> Psalm 119, verse 19, begins, "I am a stranger in the land." But why should David, the author, refer to himself as a stranger? Because, when it comes to knowledge of Torah, he does not know the difference between his right hand and his left. Now if David, who sang so many songs and so many psalms, said, "I am a stranger in the land," then it is all the more certain that *we* know nothing of the Torah. So Scripture tells us: "We are strangers before Thee, O God, as all our fathers were."

You, too, may still feel strange in the presence of the great questions. You, too, feel as though you have never even reached the first page. What, after all, can any of us say for certain about God or about our life with Him? Was all our study worthwhile? Did we really learn anything; or will our Confirmation be just a pretense to knowledge we do not have? Have we the right to decide these terrible issues when we still know so little?

The Baal Shem Tov, discussing a passage in the Talmud, helped us when we began to consider these issues: "Had they but abandoned Me," the Talmud says of God, "and kept faith with My Torah!" The Baal Shem interprets as follows:

> "They have abandoned Me," that is, they have abandoned the search to know Me, because it is not possible. But, oh, if only they had abandoned Me with searching and understanding, so keeping faith with My Torah!

Judaism is not answers! It is a life-long search for answers. Judaism is not having God, as we have a sweater or an idea or even a human friend. Judaism is the life-long search for God. Our Torah does not deliver Him to us; it merely sets us on a way, a life-long road in the right direction. Our convictions can never be proud possessions or secure knowledge; they are a part of ourselves.

Therefore, Confirmation does not claim that we have mastered Judaism. It is not an arrogant act which finishes our religious task. It is, rather, our affirmation that the Jewish road is one that we now propose to take. Confirmation is not what makes us Jews; we were Jews at birth. But Confirmation, study, decision, all these together lead up toward the kind of Jew we now shall try to be. Will Herberg wrote just a few years ago:

> . . . everything depends on decision. Every Jew is under the covenant, whether by birth or adoption; and once under the covenant, his covenant-existence is an objective fact independent of his will. He can no more help it than he can help being a man of the twentieth century or the son of his father. The son is indeed confronted with a crucial decision; to be a good son or a bad son, to live up to or to repudiate the responsibilities of sonship, but no matter what he does or desires to do, he cannot make himself not the son of his father. So, too, the Jew. He is confronted with a crucial, life-determining choice: to acknowledge and try to live up to or to repudiate the responsibilities of his Jewish convenant-existence, but no matter what he does, he cannot remove himself from under the covenant and its obligations. The fateful decision confronting every Jew is therefore not: Shall I or shall I not come under the covenant?—but: Shall I affirm my covenant-existence and live an *authentic* life or shall I deny it and as a consequence live an *inauthentic* one? Judaism is the living out of the affirmative decision. It is the decision to take the Way of the Torah.

The Mishnah reminds us that not only Judaism, but the whole world depends upon our decision. Confirmation, when we tell what we want for ourselves and what we want to be for others, is a day on which our personal decision really could rock the world:

> A single man was created in the world, to teach that if any man has caused a single soul to perish, Scripture imputes it to him as though he had caused the whole world to perish. If man saves alive a single soul, Scripture imputes it to him as though he had saved alive the whole world. . . . For man stamps many coins with the one seal and they are all like one another; but the King of Kings, the Holy One blessed is He, has stamped every man with the seal of the first man, yet not one of them is like his fellow. Therefore, everyone must say, "For my sake was the world created."

Rabbi Pinhas, like all the Hasidic teachers, emphasized that what each single person does is decisive.

> They asked Rabbi Pinhas: "Why is it written, 'In the day that God created *a* man on earth,' and not 'in the day that God created man on earth'?" He explained, "You should serve your Maker as though there were only one man on earth, only yourself."

To do this, all we have learned will be needed. The vision of all the generations will be in our eyes when we look up for blessing at our Confirmation. But we must look with our own eyes. We cannot be Jews in any way but our own. We cannot face God except as *we* are. And this means that we must do more than study and think. It means we must struggle and grow and suffer for what we believe. Hayim Greenberg, a great modern Zionist thinker, once said:

> For the modern man the way of religious renewal is the way of solitude and loneliness. Nobody can dream

his dreams for him or suffer his torments. Moses the Law-Giver, Hillel the Sage, Jesus, Francis of Assisi, Rabbi Moses Cordovera, Spinoza, and the Baal-Shem may be his supports, those who awaken and admonish him, but he will have to carve out for himself the substance and truth of religion; his "revelations" will have to be his own.

In preparing for Confirmation you have had to listen to many other people: your parents and teachers, your Rabbi, your textbooks, your older friends. You must not forget now to listen to yourself, too, because you are now the one who will decide the fate of the Jew. The prophets and the sages are dead. Even your teachers will not live on beyond your generation. They cannot save Judaism or continue it. But you can! Your life is the crucial link between the past and whatever future there might be. Abraham Heschel wrote:

In the elementary textbooks of Hebrew in use a quarter of a century ago, there was a story of a schoolboy who would be in great distress every morning, having forgotten where he put away his clothes and books before he went to bed. One evening he arrived at an answer to his problem. He wrote on a slip of paper, "The suit is on the chair, the hat is in the closet, the books on the desk, the shoes under the chair, and I am in bed." Next morning he began to collect his things together. They were all in their places. When he came to the last item on the list, he went to look for himself in the bed—but his search was in vain.

In this hour we, the living, are "the people of Israel." The tasks begun by the patriarchs and prophets and continued by their descendants, are now entrusted to us. We are either the last Jews or those who will hand over the entire past to generations to come. We will either forfeit or enrich the legacy of ages.

The Jewish world needs you. It may not be living up to the ideals it inherited nor building the future of which it dreamed. It has not always studied carefully the wisdom of the past. It is not meeting all the commands of the present. The reason is that it has lost the understanding of why the past is important and what the present could be. All of us, students and teachers, communities and Jewish men and women, must recapture the meaning of Jewish faith in order to create a Judaism worth surviving. Waldo Frank, an American Jewish writer of our century, said:

> If Jewish life is weakening, it is because the Idea of the Jew is stricken. If the Jews are less heroic than they were, it is because they no longer know why they should be heroic: it is because they no longer know why, actually, they are Jews. Whether the Idea of the Jew is stricken fatally and forever, or is in mere transition to a new substantiation, we shall not know until we do know what this Idea is.
>
> The Jewish Folk today is sick. If you would verify this in your own experience, remember that health in its lowest sense means physical and functional unity of the body, means harmony and wholeness of all its parts. Wholeness and health are one; the healthy body is that which works as a whole. Remember that social and spiritual health implies a like harmony and wholeness (not uniformity) in social, spiritual life. And now look at your own world. What harmony is there between you and your children, beyond the lowest bonds of carnal affection? What harmony in ideals, in religion, in thought, in pleasures? What harmony is there between the commands of your faith and the facts of your everyday life? Between your mood on the Day of Atonement and on a day of business? Between your amusements and your inherited arts? Between your pleasures and your

duties? What unity is there between your Rabbi reading the Torah and the Prophets, and your synagogue comfortably settled on the basis of the individual "success" of its supporters?

The contemporary American Synagogue is failing in its function as leader and healer of the Jewish Folk. There are in the Rabbinate men of high intellectual and moral will. Despite them, the Synagogue fails, because it works by a method no longer valid: It assumes that the bases of the Jewish idea are intact and that the task of Jewish leadership is still merely to interpret and substantiate the Idea to the folk. But the Idea is no longer sound; very simply because, in terms of modern thought and law and history and science, it is no longer recognized or recognizable.

If the Synagogue permanently fails, the Jewish race is doomed. By Synagogue I mean a focus for divine service by the Jews. By divine service I mean a life lived according to a religious ideal. Such a life needs a hearth for its communal expressions in thought and art. Vital Judaism will never outlive the need of what the Synagogue should be. Nor do I find a reason why the word Synagogue, with its heroic inheritance, should be discarded. It is a good word. So is God a good word, an infinitely better word than Deity, Life-force, Divine Principle and the rest of the "modern" (really eighteenth century) jargons.

It is shameful for a man to identify himself with an Idea or Spiritual Form, simply because he was born in a word-association with it. We must accept our physical inheritance. We can't help being born brown-eyed or American or French. But to be a Methodist or a Republican or an Anarchist, because I was born one, is shameful. To be a Jew merely because I was born one is equally shameful.

We cannot be Jews merely because we were born Jews. We must be *confirmed* in our Judaism, willing to live the Jewish way. This is not a matter only of studying the past. It is not only a belief or a ceremony. Franz Rosenzweig told us what it *is:*

> What we mean by Judaism, the Jewishness of the Jewish human being, is nothing that can be grasped in a religious literature or even in a religious life; nor can it be "entered" as one's "creed" in the civil registry of births, marriages, and deaths. The point is simply that it is no entity, no subject among other subjects, no one sphere of life among other spheres of life. It is something inside the individual that makes him a Jew, something infinitesimally small yet immeasurably large, his most impenetrable secret, yet evident in every gesture and every word—especially in the most spontaneous of them. The Jewishness I mean is no literature. It can be grasped through neither the writing nor the reading of books. It is not even "undergone." It is only lived—and perhaps not even that. One is it.
>
> One is Jewish!
>
> If he has prepared himself quite simply to have everything that happens to him, inwardly and outwardly, happen to him in a *Jewish way*—his vocation, his nationality, his marriage, and even, if that has to be, his Juda-"ism"—then he may be certain that with the simple assumption of that infinite pledge he will become in reality "wholly Jewish."
>
> And there is indeed no other way to become completely Jewish; the Jewish human being arises in no other way.

If we must admit that the Judaism we see all around us is not as strong or as wise as it should be, that is no reason to give up the struggle to make it wiser and stronger. It is up to us not just to take over the past, but to change it and make possible a different kind of future. Confirmation is not accepting Judaism; it is creating it.

And all around us, even in the midst of confusion,

are good men and women, brave young people who are willing to risk something to create a new Jewish way. They have wrestled, as you are wrestling, with the great questions and the great thoughts. They are beginning, as you are beginning, to add their own selves to the future. Judaism is realistic; it sees the present for what it is and does not pretend that it is better than it is. But Judaism is also optimistic; it sees the future as open to man's noblest striving. Rabbi Milton Steinberg dreamed of a richer future for the Jew:

> I see in Palestine a Jewish Commonwealth where the homeless Jews of the world have found rest, where the Jewish spirit has been reborn, whence flow to the dispersion inspiration and the stuff on which it feeds.
>
> I see the Jewries of the world, each at ease and firmly rooted in the land of its residence, each unswervingly devoted to the polity and culture of that land and at the same time the bearer and transmitter of a living Hebraism, significant to itself, its environment, and the world.
>
> Most specifically, I see an American Jewry, emancipated along with all other Americans from the restraints of prejudice, secure against violence, free to fulfill itself without hindrance.
>
> An American Jewry alight with a religious faith hallowed by antiquity and responsive to the mystery of all things, yet sanctified by the best in modern thought and clean with reasonableness.
>
> An American Jewry standing four square by Judaism's great moral ideals, sharpening them into the keenest contemporaneousness, applying them boldly, imaginatively— so that the name Jew is a synonym for the practice and advocacy of justice, compassion, freedom and peace.
>
> An American Jewry literate in both its heritages, the American and Hebraic, creative in both, cross-blending

and fertilizing the two until all devotion to one shall connote blessing for the other as well.

An American Jewry that in its observance is both reverential of the tradition and awake to current needs, so that the precious freightage of the past is enriched by new gifts in each generation.

An American Jewry whose household is set in order.

An American Jewry which, having labored that Zion be rebuilt, now draws the waters in joy from the fountain-head of the Jewish spirit.

I see in sum a Jewry which in its inner life has made Judaism what it is intended to be, what it is now in some measure, and what it can become in infinitely greater degree—that is to say, a source of blessing.

And I see all this in a new, brave and free world which Jews, together with all men of good will, have helped to set free, laboring as individuals but also as Jews, as members of a fellowship consecrated from the womb to the ideal of a new, brave and free world.

To make this dream come true, you will have to be firm in your Confirmation. You will have to grow toward Jewish insight and service. You will have to study, search, and build. But you will not be working alone. Your class, your congregation, all of our world is moving toward a future that we now only dimly see.

And God works, too. He will not leave us alone, though He also will not do our work for us. He will not destroy us when we fail, though He will not pretend our failures are not serious when they are. He will help us if we help Him to kindle that light by which both He and we are seen. For today, it may seem that God is eclipsed. But He is still there. And so are we. Martin Buber gives us a Confirmation choice which is also a command and a promise:

"Each age is, of course, a continuation of the preceding one, but a continuation can be Confirmation or it can be refutation.

Something is taking place in the depths that, as yet, needs no name. Tomorrow, even, it may happen that it will be beckoned to from the heights. The eclipse of the light of God is no extinction; even tomorrow that which has stepped in between may give way."

Notes

Notes

Chapter One: "What Must a Jew Believe?"

The Baal Shem Tov bowing his head to be blessed—in Martin Buber, *Tales of the Hasidim*, Vol. I. New York, Schocken, 1947, p. 100.

Milton Steinberg on "Creed"—Milton Steinberg, *Basic Judaism*. New York, Harcourt, Brace and Co., 1947, pp. 31-33.

"All Israelites have a share in the coming world . . ."—*Mishnah Sanhedrin* X: 1.

Philo on Dogma—cf. H. A. Wolfson, *Philo*, Cambridge, Harvard Univ. Press, 1948, Chapter III.

Creed of Maimonides—Thirteen Principles of the Faith in Hertz Daily Prayer Book, New York, Bloch Publ. Co., 1959, pp. 248-255.

Albo on "roots," "stems," and "branches"—quoted in Samuel S. Cohon, *What We Jews Believe*. Cincinnati, U.A.H.C., 1931, p. 62.

Kaufmann Kohler's beliefs—in K. Kohler's *Jewish Theology*, New York, Macmillan, 1923, pp. 19-25.

The "Columbus Platform"—in *Yearbook of the Central Conference of American Rabbis*, Vol. XLVII (1937).

"Faith in Judaism is not creed . . ."—Abba Hillel Silver, *Where Judaism Differed*. New York, Macmillan, 1957, p. 174.

Leo Baeck on "Faith"—Leo Baeck, *Dieses Volk*, Vol. I. Frankfurt am Main, Europäische Verlagsanstalt, 1955, p. 34. (Translated here from the German original by Dora Edinger and A. J. Wolf.)

The Baal Shem Tov on "Our God and God of our fathers"—quoted in Nahum N. Glatzer, *In Time and Eternity*. New York, Schocken, 1946, p. 87.

"The moment at Sinai . . ."—Abraham J. Heschel, *God in Search of Man*. Philadelphia, J.P.S., 1956 & 1959.

"The judge that shall be in those days . . ."—Talmud, Rosh Hashanah 25a, b; quoted in A. Cohen, *Everyman's Talmud*. New York, Dutton, 1949, p. 157.

The Baal Shem Tov on "Had they but abandoned Me. . . "— quoted in Nahum N. Glatzer, *In Time and Eternity*, pp. 86-87.

Chapter Two: "Is There a God?"

The post-Biblical Teachers—quoted in Abba Hillel Silver, *Where Judaism Differed*, p. 3.

Philo on Fleeing from God—quoted in Nahum N. Glatzer, *In Time and Eternity*, p. 36.

Rabbi Barukh—His Story—in Martin Buber, *Tales of the Hasidim*, I, p. 97.

Franz Rosenzweig on Truth—in Will Herberg, *Judaism and Modern Man*, Philadelphia, J.P.S., 1951, p. 36.

Abraham J. Heschel on Commitment—in *Man Is Not Alone*, Philadelphia, Jewish Publication Society, 1951, pp. 81-82.

Maimonides, on Love of God—quoted in Abraham J. Heschel, *God in Search of Man*, pp. 153-154.

K. Kohler on Reason and Intuition—*Jewish Theology*, p. 70.

Martin Buber, on Real Faith—quoted in Jacob Trapp (ed), *To Hallow This Life*, New York, Harper and Row, 1958, p. 89.

Claude G. Montefiore, on The Religion of Man—*Outlines of Liberal Judaism*, London, Macmillan, 1923, p. 21.

The Berditchever and the Unbeliever—quoted in Martin Buber, *Tales of the Hasidim*, I, pp. 228-229.

Milton Steinberg, Arguments for God's Existence—*Basic Judaism*, pp. 37-38.

Rabbi Moshe on the Fiddler—in Martin Buber, *Tales of the Hasidim*, I, p. 53.

Chapter Three: "What Is God Like?"

Talmudic quotations about the hidden secrets—in Abraham J. Heschel, *God in Search of Man*, p. 62.

Rabbi Joshua in A. Cohen, *Everyman's Talmud*, p. 3.

Mekilta on Terms for God—to Ex. XIX, 18 in A. Cohen, *Everyman's Talmud*, pp. 6-7.

The Talmud on God's Uniqueness—in A. Cohen, *Everyman's Talmud*, p. 6.

Maimonides, Against Anthropomorphism, *Guide for the Perplexed*, I.36, after the translation of M. Friedlander, New York, Hebrew Publishing Co., n. d., p. 134.

K. Kohler, on Anthropomorphisms—*Jewish Theology*, p. 76.

"The Strange Gods"—from *The Mekilta*, ed. Lauterbach, Philadelphia, J.P.S., 1933, Volume II, 239.

On God's Kinship—Claude G. Montefiore, *Outlines of Liberal Judaism*, pp. 88-89.

The Personal God of Leo Baeck, *Dieses Volk*, Vol. I, p. 114 (translated by Dora Edinger and A. J. Wolf).

The Story of The Alien—Jerusalem Talmud, Ber. 13b, quoted in A. Cohen, *Everyman's Talmud*, p. 9.

The Philosopher Hermann Cohen—in Nahum N. Glatzer, *Franz Rosenzweig*, New York, Schocken, 1953, p. 282.

God means—Abraham J. Heschel, *Man Is Not Alone*, p. 109.

God as our Ruler—Claude G. Montefiore, *Outlines of Liberal Judaism*, pp. 89-90.

The Fear of Rabbi Zusya—in Martin Buber, *Tales of the Hasidim*, I, pp. 246-247.

On Reverence—Claude G. Montefiore, *Outlines of Liberal Judaism*, p. 111.

On Fear of God—Martin Buber in Jacob Trapp (ed) *To Hallow This Life*, p. 76.

Love and Fear—Leo Baeck, *God and Man in Judaism*, New York, U.A.H.C., 1958, pp. 40-41.

Justice and Mercy—Gen. Rabbah XII, 15, in A. Cohen, *Everyman's Talmud*, p. 18.

The Song of the Berditchever—in Martin Buber, *Tales of the Hasidim*, I, p. 212.

God beyond Man—K. Kohler, *Jewish Theology*, p. 81.

The Mirror—Talmud quoted in Nahum N. Glatzer, *In Time and Eternity*, pp. 19-20.

"God said . . . ," quoted by Claude G. Montefiore and H. Loewe in *A Rabbinic Anthology*, Philadelphia, J.P.S., 1960, p. 6.

NOTES

The *Sh'ma*—from the Prayer Book.
On the *Sh'ma*—Claude G. Montefiore, *Outlines of Liberal Judaism*, pp. 49-50.
Let God in—Martin Buber, quoted in Trapp, *To Hallow This Life*, p. 3.

Chapter Four: "Why Do Good People Suffer?"

Free Will in Maimonides—quoted in Nahum N. Glatzer, *In Time and Eternity*, pp. 26, 65, and 68.
Is there any evil?—The Seer of Lublin, quoted in Martin Buber, *Tales of the Hasidim*, I, p. 318.
On Suffering—Claude G. Montefiore, *Outlines of Liberal Judaism*, pp. 71 and 141.
On vicarious Suffering—Talmud Shabbat 33b, quoted in A. Cohen, *Everyman's Talmud*, p. 125.
The Universe makes for Righteousness—Claude G. Montefiore, *Outlines of Liberal Judaism*, pp. 52-53.
God hides—Martin Buber, *At the Turning*, New York, Farrar, Straus and Young, 1952, pp. 59-60.
The theories of Suffering—Milton Steinberg, *Basic Judaism*, pp. 54-55.
Give thanks for Suffering—The Mekilta, quoted in A. Cohen, *Everyman's Talmud*, p. 127.
Live through Suffering—Abba Hillel Silver, *Where Judaism Differed*, p. 116.

Chapter Five: "Why Pray?"

The rules for Prayer—Talmud Ber. 31a, 30b and Yeb. 105b—in A. Cohen, *Everyman's Talmud*, pp. 88, 91.
Cry to God—The Maggid, quoted in Martin Buber, *Tales of the Hasidim*, I, p. 103.
Rabbi Simeon in Sayings of the Fathers, translated by Judah Goldin in *The Living Talmud*, N.Y. Mentor Books, New American Library, 1957, p. 112.
Two kinds of Prayer—Abraham J. Heschel, *Man's Quest for God*, N.Y. Scribner's, 1954, pp. 27-28.

The pious men of old—Ber. V, 1—in A. Cohen, *Everyman's Talmud*, p. 22.

On Concentration in Prayer—Maimonides, *Moreh Nebukim* III, 51.

The Teacher, quoted in Martin Buber, *Tales of the Hasidim*, I, p. 269.

The Watchmaker—by Israel Friedman, quoted in Abraham J. Heschel, *Man's Quest for God*, pp. 36-37.

Prayer as Communion—Claude G. Montefiore, *Outlines of Liberal Judaism*, pp. 98-99.

The Effect upon God—Martin Buber in Trapp, *To Hallow This Life*, pp. 85-86.

God hears—Exodus Rabba XXI, 3 in A. Cohen, *Everyman's Talmud*, p. 87.

Rabbi Susia—quoted in Nahum N. Glatzer, *In Time and Eternity*, p. 62.

Chapter Six: "Is the Bible True?"

Ben Bag Bag on Torah—in Sayings of the Fathers, Translated by Judah Goldin in *The Living Talmud*, p. 223.

To the modern Reader—Nahum N. Glatzer, *Franz Rosenzweig*, p. 258.

Rabbi Jacob J. Weinstein, *The Place of Understanding*, New York, Bloch, 1958, pp. 8-9.

"Human Substance . . ."—Buber, in Jacob Trapp, *To Hallow This Life*, p. 112.

Inspiration errs—Claude G. Montefiore, *Outlines in Liberal Judaism*, p. 215.

We must be present—Abraham J. Heschel, *God in Search of Man*, pp. 252-253.

The Heathen before Hillel and Shammai—Shabbat 31a, in A. Cohen, *Everyman's Talmud*, p. 155.

Sages Heirs of the Prophets—Baba Bathra 12a, in A. Cohen, *Everyman's Talmud*, p. 131.

Moses before Akiba—quoted in Claude G. Montefiore and H. Loewe, *A Rabbinic Anthology*, London, 1938, p. 217.

The Maggid interprets a dream—in Martin Buber, *Tales of the Hasidim*, I, p. 110.

The Bible is true—Abraham J. Heschel, *God in Search of Man,* pp. 199 and 247.

"He who says . . ."—Sanhedrin X, 1, in A. Cohen, *Everyman's Talmud,* p. 154.

The Torah is human—Samuel S. Cohon, *What We Jews Believe,* p. 116.

"We differ with Orthodoxy. . . ."—Franz Rosenzweig, quoted in Will Herberg, *Judaism and Modern Man,* p. 249.

Rabbi Levi Yitzhak's Answer—quoted in Martin Buber, *Tales of the Hasidim,* I, p. 232.

Chapter Seven: "Why Aren't We Christians?"

On Jesus—Leo Baeck, *Judaism and Christianity,* Philadelphia, J.P.S., 1958, pp. 100 and following.

On Jesus' teachings—Claude G. Montefiore, *Outlines of Liberal Judaism,* p. 331.

Messiah has not come—Isaac Troki, *Hizzuk Emunah* I.2, 4a, 6, quoted in the Jewish Encyclopedia, IV, 57.

Judaism is superior—K. Kohler, *Jewish Theology,* p. 17.

Judaism is Mitzvah—A. J. Heschel, quoted in David Aronson, *The Jewish Way of Life,* New York, United Synagogue, 1957, pp. 35-36.

Jewish Doctrine is nobler—Claude G. Montefiore, *Outlines of Liberal Judaism,* pp. 319-320.

The fork of the road—Abba Hillel Silver, *Where Judaism Differed,* pp. 106-107.

Abraham and Sarah—Rabbi Elazar, quoted by Claude G. Montefiore and H. Loewe, *A Rabbinic Anthology,* p. 570.

Repel and accept—Rabbi Samuel, quoted by Claude G. Montefiore and H. Loewe, *A Rabbinic Anthology,* p. 578.

Why Religions differ—Joseph Albo, quoted in Samuel S. Cohon, *What We Jews Believe,* pp. 27-28.

Christian Morality—J. Emden, *Resen Mat'eh,* 15b, quoted in the Jewish Encyclopedia, IV, 57.

The Mission of Christianity—Nahum N. Glatzer, *Franz Rosenzweig,* p. 341.

A Democratic Nation—Waldo Frank, *The Jew In Our Day,* New York, Duell, Sloan & Pearce, 1944, pp. 36-37.

Jesus preaches Monotheism—Maimonides: *Mishneh Torah, M'lakim* xi. 4.

Chapter Eight: "Science and Religion"

"Whoever says . . ."—Rabbi Pinhas—quoted in Martin Buber, *Tales of the Hasidim*, I, p. 134.
The Sages were not scientists—Maimoides, adapted from Ben Zion Bokser, *The Legacy of Maimonides*, New York, Phil. Library, 1950, pp. 62-63.
Maimonides on Miracles—Comment on Sayings of the Fathers—Translated by Judah Goldin in *The Living Talmud*, p. 194.
The Rabbis' View of Miracles, Talmud, *Baba Metzia*, 59b.
The World is Law—Claude G. Montefiore, *Outlines of Liberal Judaism*, pp. 84-85.
We are the Miracle—K. Kohler, *Jewish Theology*, p. 166.
Elijah's Miracle—Rabbi Barukh—quoted in Martin Buber, *Tales of the Hasidim*, I, p. 93.
On Maimonides—The Rizhyner—quoted in Martin Buber, *Tales of the Hasidim*, II, p. 58.
On Evolution—Claude G. Montefiore, *Outlines of Liberal Judaism*, p. 117.
Reason and Faith—Abraham J. Heschel, *Man Is Not Alone*, p. 173.
God let us unravel—Claude G. Montefiore, *Outlines of Liberal Judaism*, p. 27.
"A new learning," Franz Rosenzweig—quoted in Nahum N. Glatzer, *Franz Rosenzweig*, p. 231.

Chapter Nine: "Ceremonies and Commandments"

"Greater is He . . ."—Rabbi Hanina: Talmud, *Kid.* 31a.
The Covenant—Nehemiah, Chapter 10.
The Ten Commandments—Exodus, Chapter 20.
Why did God choose us?—*Numbers Rabba*, XIV.10 and *Sifre Deut.*, 343, 142b, quoted in A. Cohen, *Everyman's Talmud*, p. 65.
God forced us—Talmud, *Shabbat*, 88a, quoted in A. Cohen, *Everyman's Talmud*, p. 66.

Why does God care?—Claude G. Montefiore and H. Loewe, *A Rabbinic Anthology*, p. 149.

Commandments purify—Talmud, *Yeb.* 20a.

The Dead does not defile—Claude G. Montefiore and H. Loewe, *A Rabbinic Anthology*, p. 150.

Each man must choose—Lubliner in Martin Buber, *Tales of the Hasidim*, I, p. 313.

The Reason for Observance—Milton Steinberg, *Basic Judaism*, pp. 136-139.

Reconstructionism on Ritual—*Toward a Guide for Jewish Ritual Usage*, New York, Reconstructionist Foundation, 1941.

Reform Judaism on Ritual—Rabbi Morton M. Berman, *Report of the Committee on Reform Practice to UAHC*, Nov. 1950; 41st General Assembly.

On Customs and Ceremonies—Abraham J. Heschel, *Man's Quest for God*, pp. 113-114.

The unfinished Commandment—Leo Baeck, *God and Man in Judaism*, p. 45.

Man's Duty—Joseph Karo, *Shulchan Aruch*, quoted in Nahum N. Glatzer, *In Time and Eternity*, p. 74.

Franz Rosenzweig—From a letter of March 27, 1922, in *Briefe*, Berlin, Schocken, 1935, transl. by Dora Edinger and Arnold J. Wolf.

Doppelt-Polish, *A Guide for Reform Jews*, N.Y. Bloch, 1957, p. 41.

Chapter Ten: "An End: a Beginning"

We are shaken—*The Midrash on Psalms*, translated by William Braude, New Haven, Yale, 1959, II, pp. 258-259.

"They have abandoned Me . . ."—The Baal Shem Tov: quoted in Nahum N. Glatzer, *In Time and Eternity*, pp. 86-87.

Everything depends on decision—Will Herberg: *Judaism and Modern Man*, p. 301.

"A single Man"—Mishnah, quoted in Will Herberg, *Judaism and Modern Man*, p. 100.

You are the only man—Rabbi Pinhas, quoted in Martin Buber, *Tales of the Hasidim*, I, p. 124.

The Way of Solitude—Hayim Greenberg, *The Inner Eye*, New York, Jewish Frontier, 1953, p. 118.

The boy who forgot—Abraham J. Heschel, *The Earth is the Lord's*, New York, Schuman, 1950, pp. 106-107.

The Idea of the Jew—Waldo Frank, *The Jew in Our Day*, New York, Duell, Sloan and Pearce, 1944, pp. 45-47.

"One is Jewish"—Nahum N. Glatzer, *Franz Rosenzweig*, pp. 215-216, and 222-223.

The Future—Milton Steinberg, quoted in David Aronson, *The Jewish Way of Life*, pp. 213-214.

The Eclipse—Martin Buber, *Eclipse of God*, New York, Harper and Row, 1957, p. 129.

An Afterword

This book began in the classroom of my uncle and teacher, Rabbi Felix Levy, twenty-five years ago. It was he who unlocked for me and for two generations of young people the treasury of Jewish religious thought. At the Hebrew Union College our teachers enabled us to search out traditional questions with more elaborate equipment, and my friends, Eugene Borowitz and Steven Schwarzschild, began a life-long colloquy with me. To them I owe an incalculable personal debt as well as whatever is worthwhile in this book.

At the Isaac M. Wise Temple, under the patient compulsion of Celia S. Singer, we initiated a program of theology for teenagers with partial but inspiriting results. To my students there, at Temple Emanuel and B'nai Jehoshua in Chicago, and Congregation Solel in Highland Park, this book is dedicated. They are the questions to whom these answers are addressed.

My approach to Jewish theology is heavily indebted to Martin Buber whose insight I have attempted to bring to Jewish young people for the first time. Dr. Dora Edinger has helped me through the intricacies of German Jewish thought. My hope is that this introduction will encourage a new generation to search out the depths of our religious thinking, and thus to continue the work which God has given our people. I have sought here to be a vessel through which tradition, old and new, can move, rather than a voice crying out its own word.

A. J. W.